Comprehensive

ACUTE TRAUMATIC STRESS MANAGEMENT™
—— CATSM ——

D1227592

a publication of

The American Academy of Experts in Traumatic Stress®

New York

Published by

The American Academy of Experts in Traumatic Stress®

Administrative Offices, 368 Veterans Memorial Highway, Commack, New York 11725
Tel. (631) 543-2217 • Fax (631) 543-6977
www.atsm.org • www.traumatic-stress.org • www.aaets.org

ISBN: 0-9674762-7-5

Comprehensive
ACUTE TRAUMATIC STRESS MANAGEMENT™
—— CATSM ——

a publication of

The American Academy of Experts in Traumatic Stress®

The American Academy of Experts in Traumatic Stress is a multidisciplinary network of professionals committed to the advancement of intervention for survivors of trauma. The Academy's international membership includes individuals from over 200 professions in the health-related fields, emergency services, criminal justice, forensics, law, business and education. With Members in every state of the United States and over 55 foreign countries, the Academy is now the largest organization of its kind in the world. For information about Membership, the International Registry, the Academy's Board Certification Programs in Traumatic Stress Specialties, Certification in Acute Traumatic Stress Management (ATSM), the Diplomate Credential, Fellowship and other benefits of Membership with the Academy, please contact:

The American Academy of Experts in Traumatic Stress®

Administrative Offices, 368 Veterans Memorial Highway, Commack, New York 11725
Tel. (631) 543-2217 • Fax (631) 543-6977
www.atsm.org • www.traumatic-stress.org • www.aaets.org

Comprehensive Acute Traumatic Stress Management is published by The American Academy of Experts in Traumatic Stress. The ATSM/CATSM model is offered with the understanding that the Academy does not practice medicine or psychology, or provide direct or indirect patient/client care. Additional copies may be obtained by utilizing the order form provided in the back of this publication.

ADMINISTRATION AND MEMBERS OF THE BOARD OF SCIENTIFIC & PROFESSIONAL ADVISORS

Table of Contents

Table of Contents (continued)

Trauma Response® Infosheets™

Application & Examination for
Certification in Acute Traumatic Stress Management
About The American Academy of Experts in Traumatic Stress
Excerpts from *Trauma Response*® Profiles

Order Form

Preface

A young man was injured in an accident at work. Twenty-three of his co-workers looked on in horror. A call was placed to 911. When paramedics arrived, they immediately addressed the young man's physical and safety needs—and transported him to the hospital for continued medical care. For this man and his co-workers, the event was over... or was it? Who addressed his emergent *psychological* needs—and the needs of those who witnessed the event? What steps were taken to address the organization's needs? The answers to these questions are found in *Comprehensive Acute Traumatic Stress Management* (CATSM).

During times of crisis, we are quick to address "physical trauma." We don't wait to call for help, and emergency medical personnel certainly don't wait to transport someone to the hospital before efforts are made to control bleeding. Unfortunately, a "hidden trauma" is often ignored. This trauma leaves the deepest scars and changes people forever—*traumatic stress*.

At the turn of the century, in our pre-September 11th world, Acute Traumatic Stress Management (ATSM) was born (Lerner and Shelton, 2001). ATSM was developed to provide emergency responders with a *Traumatic Stress Response Protocol*. It was designed to raise the level of care—beyond traditional emergency medical intervention. It enabled first responders to address emergent *psychological* needs.

There were many lessons learned after September 11th. One of them was the realization that crises do not always have a beginning and an end—and, that traumatic stress can impact individuals, groups, organizations, communities—even an entire nation. We have all observed how traumatic stress disables people, causes disease, precipitates mental disorders, leads to substance abuse, and destroys relationships and families.

Traumatic stress is experienced by survivors of disasters and catastrophes (e.g., hurricanes, airplane crashes, terrorist bombings, train derailments, and floods). However, it does not have to take a highly publicized event to cause debilitating emotional scars. Traumatic stress has many "faces," and is experienced every day during and in the aftermath of our *personal* tragedies (e.g., facing a serious illness, dealing with the loss of a loved one, experiencing an automobile accident, etc.).

Much has been written about crisis intervention—"psychological first-aid" introduced in the aftermath of a tragedy. Notwithstanding, there is little information offering practical strategies to help people *during* a traumatic event. This is a time when people are perhaps most suggestible and vulnerable to traumatic stress—a tremendous opportunity for intervention.

ATSM offers "practical tools" for addressing the wide spectrum of traumatic experiences—from mild to the most severe. It is a goal-directed process delivered within the framework of a facilitative or helping attitudinal climate. ATSM aims to "jump-start" an individual's coping and problem-solving abilities. It seeks to stabilize acute symptoms of traumatic stress and stimulate healthy, adaptive functioning. Finally, ATSM may increase the likelihood of an individual pursuing mental health intervention, if need be, in the future.

ATSM offers techniques for connecting with particularly challenging, emotionally distraught, individuals. It helps us to help others when time is limited and to know what to say when we are at a loss for words. It helps us while intervening with diverse populations such as children, sexual assault victims, potentially violent and substance-involved individuals, as well as depressed and potentially suicidal people. It provides a strategy to support grieving individuals and offers an application to address serious injury/death notification. Finally, ATSM addresses our own responses during a crisis.

We know that people who are exposed to traumatic events experience the "Imprint of Horror"—the sights, sounds, smells, tastes and tactile sensations that are recorded in one's mind during a traumatic event. These perceptions precipitate acute traumatic stress reactions and chronic stress disorders. In the same way that these negative stimuli can be etched in peoples' minds during traumatic exposure—a period of heightened suggestibility and vulnerability, so too may the positive, adaptive forces of ATSM (e.g., active listening, empathic understanding, a supportive presence, etc.).

Comprehensive Acute Traumatic Stress Management (CATSM) reflects the expansion of the ATSM model by addressing the emergent psychological needs of individuals, groups and organizations before, during and after a traumatic event. CATSM is a *Traumatic Stress Response Protocol* for all people who endeavor to help others during times of crisis. By reaching people early, we can keep individuals and organizations functioning, and mitigate long-term emotional suffering.

Mark D. Lerner, Ph.D.
Raymond D. Shelton, Ph.D.

CHAPTER ONE

Introduction

The day was beautiful, typical for late May. Except for the forecast of possible late day thunderstorms, nothing was out of the ordinary for this time of year. At about 3pm the sky began to darken, hinting at the possibility that the weather service might be on track with their earlier prediction of storms.

Most people in the town paid little attention to the sky. Thunderstorms during this time of year are common. However, the sky on this day seemed to be turning rather quickly. It had a more ominous appearance than usual. At about 3:45 the weather service issued a severe storm warning for the area, stating that the probability of severe weather, strong winds, cloud to ground lightening and hail was possible through 5pm. The typical statement of seek shelter was given.

This town has a population of 18,000. Mostly a farming and ranch community with a medium sized auto part manufacturing plant employing 800 people. The homes are wood frame construction developments and there are two mobile home parks. There is one small shopping mall, 5 schools, 6 churches, 2 synagogues and a small community hospital. Emergency services consist of a 225 member volunteer fire department with 3 basic life support EMT staffed ambulances and one advanced life support ambulance staffed with two paramedics per tour. The police department is 128 members strong.

For all practical purposes this community is typical middle America with hard working people. It is comprised of young families raising children and building careers and some retired and elderly individuals. A community that exists everyday without notice – that is without notice until something happens to make the world aware of its existence.

The weather continued to deteriorate. At 4:19pm a severe thunder cell had developed, producing heavy rain, hail, and cloud to ground lightening. The weather service issued another bulletin stating the danger and possibility of tornados developing. Residents were warned to be on the lookout for funnel shaped clouds and to seek shelter immediately. The wind had begun to gust significantly. The storm was on a southeast course, moving at 15mph; it was heading directly for the town.

At 4:30 a funnel cloud touched ground 1 mile southeast of town. Within 2 minutes, the tornado, estimated at a category 4 slammed into the auto plant on the edge of town. The impact collapsed the roof and corner of the building killing 5 workers, pinning 6, and injuring an additional 32.

The tornado continued its destruction cutting a path through one of the mobile home parks destroying 18 mobile homes and injuring 12 people, 5 critically. Fortunately, no one died in this section of town.

The storm turned sharply to the north where it impacted a fire substation, destroying it and the engine and ladder trucks that were quartered there. As the tornado continued to move on its northerly track it destroyed 3 more homes and the local radio station tower. The final damage occurred when the tornado struck a farm, destroying the barn, killing 10 horses and the farmers' three dogs. The farmhouse sustained moderate damage.

In a matter of 8 minutes, this peaceful, happy community suffered devastating loss and destruction. As the winds died out and the rain subsided, it became safe to come out of shelter. The effect of the storm immediately impacted the residents. Shock and disbelief were evident. People were dazed, disoriented and confused. The strong peripheral winds had created significant damage to buildings and homes. The first vision people had was of a very different landscape. The sense of normalcy was lost.

Engagement

In the immediate moments following the tornados path through town, activity was slow to begin. People stood and looked around not believing what had just occurred. Slowly the realization of the magnitude of the event began to set in.

At the auto plant, screams could be heard. Some of the screams were of physical pain and acute emotional distress; some were frantic screams for help from people trapped in the rubble. At the mobile home park, the devastation was complete. People stood in horror, trying to grasp what had occurred. Some wandered aimlessly amidst the ruin of their home, some searched for loved ones they could not locate. As the moments went by, the horror began to set in.

Within 5 minutes of the storms departure, the fire department began its response. However, very quickly they began to realize they were overwhelmed, a reaction not familiar to emergency responders. They were down two pieces of apparatus from the destroyed substation, were severely undermanned and, in the departments history, had never faced an event of this magnitude. They divided their response sending units to the sites most severely hit by the tornado. One young fire officer stated that as they rolled up to the auto plant, he recalled looking at the collapsed roof and portion of the building, saw people running toward the truck, screaming at him to help the trapped people. He remembered "drawing a blank," and not being able to formulate a plan of action. He believed it must have been 2-3 minutes before he could comprehend what he was seeing and take action. The chief called for mutual aid.

At the hospital, people began to wander in with varying degrees of injury. Some were carried in, some walked in on their own. Initially, the injuries being seen were minor; however, the numbers of patients quickly began to overwhelm the emergency department. Nurses in the ER stated that while the medical needs of the patients were not critical, the emotional trauma was. One nurse stated, "I was completely secure in my ability to tend to the injuries; however, I did not have a clue as to how to approach the emotional pain." Her feeling was echoed over and over by hospital staff including physicians, lab, office, security and other personnel.

The clergy responded, attempting to attend to the emotional needs of their people. In some cases it was just their presence that helped. Others required a more intense connection. In one case, a minister reported seeing a woman sitting on a refrigerator that was in the road. As he approached her, he realized she was holding a picture of her daughter. When he asked her if she was okay, she stated "I can't find my little girl." He said, "I sat down with her, put my arm around her and realized that for the first time in my many years of ministry—I did not know what to say."

Within 20 minutes, assistance began to arrive from surrounding communities. Additional fire service, police, and mobile disaster units began to relieve some of the burden on the town's emergency responders and hospital staff. This would be a long, intense, dark night—there was no electricity. Fear and a powerful feeling of disconnection and aloneness would be present. Tomorrow would bring new challenge, as this town would start its road to recovery.

The Aftermath

The town began to stabilize as disaster services arrived. Medical support, sanitation, food service, fire / EMS and police presence was improved. The town's clergy provided emotional and spiritual support and opened the doors to their churches and synagogues for shelter.

Within 12 hours, Catastrophe Response Teams from various insurance companies began to arrive. They would signify the "new beginning," their work was necessary for rebuilding to occur. Mobile office space was set up in order for claims adjusters to meet with their clients, a process these team members have been through before. One team member mentioned that no matter how many times he has responded to disasters, he is never able to get used to what he sees, nor the people's emotional pain.

At the auto parts plant, 5 people had died and 32 were injured. The building had sustained severe damage and would be unable to resume operations for some time. This further impacted the community by preventing the large amount of staff from returning to work, creating an economic issue. The impact on staff was enormous and would require a complete restructuring within the organization to rebuild physically and emotionally from this incident. It would take more than "bricks and mortar" to stabilize and return to a normal state of function.

The total loss of life from this tornado was 18, 4 of which were children, the youngest being 3 months. Funeral services for these town members would severely challenge the two funeral directors who found themselves overwhelmed with the loss. Ultimately, these men and their staff would require psychological support following the work they had to do.

Over the course of weeks, the town began to regroup and rebuild. The evidence of the physical damage the storm had created slowly disappeared. Services were back online and even the auto plant was able to begin moderate operations. The resilience of the human spirit was evident; failure was not an option. This town would rise again.

However, while the physical wounds were being repaired quickly, the emotional trauma remained. There were significant losses to grieve of family, friends, pets and a way of life. The tornado had lasted 5 minutes, the recovery would last a lifetime.

When we experience a traumatic event, there is always a rush to address our "physical trauma." The problem is, whether we are physically hurt or not, a "hidden trauma" is often ignored. This trauma leaves the deepest scars and changes us forever. *Acute Traumatic Stress Management* addresses the hidden trauma—traumatic stress.

What is traumatic stress?

Traumatic stress refers to the emotional, cognitive, behavioral, physiological and spiritual experience of individuals who are exposed to, or who witness, events that overwhelm their coping and problem-solving abilities. These events, sometimes referred to as "critical incidents," are typically unexpected and uncontrollable. They compromise our sense of safety and security, and leave us feeling insecure and vulnerable.

Traumatic stress disables people, causes disease, precipitates mental disorders, leads to substance abuse, and destroys relationships and families. In organizations, traumatic stress leads to communication breakdowns, a decrease in morale and group cohesiveness, excessive absenteeism, an increase in health care costs, workers' compensation and disability claims, an inability to retain effective personnel and, ultimately, a marked decrease in productivity.

Traumatic stress is not Posttraumatic Stress Disorder (PTSD). The former is a normal response to an abnormal event. PTSD is a psychiatric disorder applied to those individuals who continue to experience a host of disturbing symptoms after exposure to an extreme traumatic stressor. According to the National Center for Posttraumatic Stress Disorder, nearly eight percent of Americans will experience PTSD at one point in their lives, with women being twice as likely to develop PTSD than men. Individuals with PTSD often experience recurrent and intrusive distressing recollections of the event, distressing dreams, "flashbacks" (i.e., acting or feeling as if the event were recurring), difficulty concentrating, hypervigilance, an exaggerated startle response, and a host of avoidance behaviors.

The bottom line—early efforts must be made to prevent debilitating "emotional scars" from negatively coloring people's lives. Ultimately, the implementation of a *Traumatic Stress Response Protocol*, within the framework of well-established emergency response procedures, will better address the needs of the "whole person" and prevent acute stress reactions from becoming chronic stress disorders.

Who experiences traumatic stress?

Traumatic stress is experienced by survivors of disasters and catastrophes (e.g., earthquakes, hurricanes, airplane crashes, terrorist attacks, train derailments, and floods). However, it does not have to take a highly publicized event with a two-inch headline to cause significant stress. Traumatic stress has many "faces," and is experienced every day during and in the aftermath of our *personal* tragedies (e.g., facing a serious illness, dealing with the loss of a loved one, experiencing an automobile accident, etc.). Early identification and intervention may ultimately prevent debilitating stress disorders.

> Ultimately, the implementation of a *Traumatic Stress Response Protocol*, within the framework of well-established emergency response procedures, will better address the needs of the "whole person."

Is traumatic stress usually caused by "severe" events?

Generally, as the severity of a traumatic event increases, so does the level of traumatic stress. For example, when arriving at the home of a 7 year-old boy who fell while climbing a tree, police officers may expect to find the child's parents stressed by what appears to be a fractured ankle. However, if the child had struck his head, was unconscious, and bleeding heavily from his nose and mouth, one may expect a greater level of traumatic stress.

Events that are particularly gruesome, such as severe burns, dismemberment, open wounds and viewing the dead will leave a powerful impact on those who the witness the incident. Similarly, the sounds of people screaming and the smell of deployed air bags will leave a lasting impression. These perceptions collectively create what may be termed the "Imprint of Horror," and are often precipitators for posttraumatic stress reactions in the hours, days and months following the event.

Although the severity of the event may be one of the most important predictors of traumatic stress, it is important to recognize that *all* traumatic events have the potential to cause significant damage. When an individual telephones 911 to request help, he is experiencing some degree of traumatic stress. It would seem that the level of stress that is precipitated by a parking lot "fender bender" could hardly compare with the experience of an assault victim. However, the severity of the event is only one factor in identifying who will ultimately manifest a debilitating stress disorder. For example, for an individual who has a history of mental illness, substance abuse and prior traumatic exposure, even a seemingly mild incident may trigger a highly maladaptive response.

What factors influence how people respond to traumatic events?

The manner in which an individual responds to a traumatic event will be based upon many variables including *pre-trauma factors* (e.g., a history of mental illness, prior traumatic exposure, substance abuse, etc.), *characteristics of the traumatic event* (e.g., the severity, proximity, intentionally caused vs. natural disaster, etc.), and *post-trauma factors* (e.g., having the opportunity to "tell his story," level of familial support, etc.). These variables, in concert with individual characteristics, will ultimately determine how a person will respond in the face of trauma. The personal meaning that an individual ascribes to a traumatic event will also influence the individual's response.

What reactions are typically exhibited *during* traumatic exposure?

When people experience traumatic events, we are quick to assess their acute physical difficulties (e.g., obstructed airway, cardiac arrest, significant blood loss, etc.). It is critical that we also understand and appreciate emergent psychological difficulties. The following emotional, cognitive, behavioral, physiological and spiritual reactions are frequently observed during traumatic exposure. Not every response is evidenced by everyone and the order in which responses are exhibited will vary from person to person.

Emotional Responses may include shock, in which the individual may present a highly anxious, active response or perhaps a seemingly stunned, emotionally-numb response. He may describe feeling as though he is "in a fog." He may exhibit denial, in which there is an inability to acknowledge the impact of the situation or perhaps, that the situation has occurred. He may evidence dissociation, in which he may seem dazed and apathetic, and he may express feelings of unreality. Other frequently observed acute emotional responses may include panic, fear, intense feelings of aloneness, hopelessness, helplessness, emptiness, uncertainty, horror, terror, anger, hostility, irritability, depression, grief and feelings of guilt.

Cognitive Responses to traumatic exposure are often reflected in impaired concentration, confusion, disorientation, difficulty in making a decision, a short attention span, suggestibility, vulnerability, forgetfulness, self-blame, blaming others, lowered self-efficacy, thoughts of losing control, hypervigilance, and perseverative thoughts of the traumatic event. For example, upon extrication of a survivor from an automobile accident, he may cognitively still "be in" the automobile "playing the tape" of the accident over and over in his mind.

Behavioral Responses in the face of a traumatic event may include withdrawal, "spacing-out," non-communication, changes in speech patterns, regressive behaviors, erratic movements, impulsivity, a reluctance to abandon property, seemingly aimless walking, pacing, an inability to sit still, an exaggerated startle response and antisocial behaviors.

Physiological Responses may include rapid heart beat, elevated blood pressure, difficulty breathing*, shock symptoms*, chest pains*, cardiac palpitations*, muscle tension and pains, fatigue, fainting, flushed face, pale appearance, chills, cold clammy skin, increased sweating, thirst, dizziness, vertigo, hyperventilation, headaches, grinding of teeth, twitches and gastrointestinal upset.   ** Require immediate medical evaluation*

It is important to recognize that these emotional, cognitive, behavioral, physiological and spiritual reactions do not necessarily represent an unhealthy or maladaptive response to a traumatic event.

21

Spiritual Responses to a traumatic incident often include anger and a distance from God. There may be a withdrawal from attending religious services. Sometimes the opposite of these reactions is experienced with a sudden turn toward God and uncharacteristic involvement in religious community activity. Additional reactions may include faith practice (e.g., prayers, scriptures, hymns, worship, communion), as empty and without meaning. There is often a belief that God is powerless, doesn't care or has failed to protect creating a questioning of one's basic beliefs. There is often anger at clergy.

It is important to recognize that these emotional, cognitive, behavioral, physiological and spiritual reactions do not necessarily represent an unhealthy or maladaptive response to a traumatic event. Rather, they may be viewed as normal responses to an abnormal event. When these reactions are experienced in the future (i.e., weeks, months or even years after the event), are joined by other symptoms (e.g., recurrent distressing dreams, "flashbacks," avoidance behaviors, etc.), and interfere with social, occupational or other important areas of functioning, a psychiatric disorder may be in evidence.

How can *we* address traumatic stress?

Current theories on crisis intervention, or "psychological first-aid," place great emphasis on disaster mental health, working with groups of people, and helping to restore a healthy adaptive way of functioning in the aftermath of a crisis. Interventions have been developed for "demobilizing," "defusing" and "debriefing" people after disengagement from a crisis—following a traumatic experience.

At the turn of this century, *Acute Traumatic Stress Management* (ATSM) was introduced (Lerner and Shelton, 2001). It was built on an empirically-based foundation that stressed the importance of addressing emergent psychological needs within the framework of a *facilitative attitudinal climate*. ATSM provided a "road map," a *Traumatic Stress Response Protocol* for emergency responders. It enabled first responders to look beyond the physical and safety needs of people and also address emergent psychological needs *during* traumatic exposure.

The introduction of *Comprehensive Acute Traumatic Stress Management* (CATSM) reflects the expansion of the ATSM model by addressing traumatic stress before, during and after a crisis. It empowers *all* caregivers with a pragmatic process that may be utilized with individuals, groups and organizations. CATSM's fundamental goal is to keep people functioning and mitigate long-term emotional suffering.

Traditional emergency response protocol dictates that immediate action be taken to change a presenting condition. However, in addressing the emergent psychological needs of individuals who have been exposed to traumatic events, we do not strive to change the presenting condition. We do not console people, lessen the pain of a loss, or work to make them feel better. We must be careful not to encourage denial or a suppression of thoughts and feelings. Rather, we aim to "jump-start" an individual's coping and problem-solving abilities. Ultimately, our goal is to help people to move through a *normal* process in the face of an *abnormal* event.

> **Ultimately, our goal is to help people to move through a *normal* process in the face of an *abnormal* event.**

We know that people who are exposed to trauma experience the "Imprint of Horror"—the sights, sounds, smells, tastes and tactile sensations that are recorded in one's mind during a traumatic event. These perceptions often precipitate acute traumatic stress reactions and chronic stress disorders. In the same way that these negative stimuli can be etched in people's minds during traumatic exposure—a period of heightened suggestibility and vulnerability, so too may the positive, adaptive forces of ATSM (e.g., active listening, empathic understanding, a supportive presence, etc.).

This *Traumatic Stress Response Protocol* empowers all caregivers with a practical strategy to address the emergent psychological needs of others before, during and after a traumatic event.

CHAPTER TWO

Comprehensive Acute Traumatic Stress Management

At a manufacturing plant located in the Midwest, an employee of 17 years was noted by his immediate line supervisor to arrive late for work on an increasing basis. In addition, his work product began to have errors and some of his work needed to be repaired. He was further observed to be short tempered and irritable with coworkers.

This employee had been the ideal staff member. Most days he was early for his shift, accurate and complete in his work and never a discipline problem. He was the staff member every manager wanted.

His line supervisor observed the negative behavior for a period of time, and finally, having enough, he decided to take action. He called the worker into his office and proceeded to reprimand him for his lateness, carelessness and poor attitude. Further, he told him that if there were no change, action would be taken.

Over the course of the next two weeks, the behavior did not improve. It was decided that he needed to be dealt with at a higher level. A meeting was setup with the line supervisor and the division manager, the staff member was called to the office for a "formal counseling."

During the session he was told that his 17 years with the company mattered little if he couldn't get his "act" together. He was being formally placed on probation and if in the next two weeks there wasn't a drastic change in attitude and performance he was "out of here."

During the barrage of negative comments and threats his eyes began to tear, he broke down and began to sob. Slowly as he regained his composure, he shared that his 14-year-old son had been diagnosed with cancer. There was not a person in the workplace that knew of this issue in his life, least of all his line manager. He was a man who was very private, and, while he would talk with coworkers on breaks and mealtime, he never talked about his life outside of the job.

The behavior and performance issues were a direct result of traumatic stress. The lack of knowledge of stress reactions, and their effect on performance on the part of his line supervisor prevented appropriate managerial action from being taken. The line supervisor reacted to the presenting behavior, never considering the cause. He missed a critical opportunity to open a supportive door that would lead toward assistance during this time of need.

To the untrained, unprepared line supervisor and division manager, the presenting behavior of this long-time employee indicated "poor attitude," and a negative work ethic. Unable to see beyond the presenting problem, they could make the only logical conclusion available—this was a discipline issue that needed threatening action to correct. Had a **Comprehensive Acute Traumatic Stress Management** *program been in place in the company, managers and staff would have been prepared to recognize and respond appropriately to the staff member's crisis. Through training, management and staff would understand the powerful nature of stress/traumatic stress and appropriate intervention could have been provided.*

What is Comprehensive Acute Traumatic Stress Management?

Comprehensive Acute Traumatic Stress Management (CATSM) is a pragmatic process that addresses the emergent psychological needs of individuals, groups and organizations experiencing traumatic stress associated with a wide spectrum of traumatic events (e.g., accidents, illness, criminal victimization, natural disasters, domestic violence, workplace violence, loss, etc.). CATSM is an integrated, multi-component program for the provision of crisis and disaster mental health services. CATSM may be viewed as a series of "practical tools" that provide a framework for managers, supervisors, educators, administrators, emergency responders, clergy, medical and healthcare personnel, catastrophe response teams and other individuals who find themselves in a position to assist victims of crises. The uniqueness of CATSM is that it is a process-oriented approach that aims to reach people *before, during* and *after* a traumatic event.

The core mission of CATSM is to establish connections between caregivers, individuals and groups of people who have been exposed to a traumatic event. It is a facilitative process that additionally fosters healthy, adaptive communication within organizations faced with a traumatic event.

CATSM recognizes the importance of pre-incident planning and education to effectively manage traumatic events. Expanding upon the basic Acute Traumatic Stress Management (ATSM) model, outlined in Chapter Three, CATSM's early intervention training provides a framework for caregivers to address the emergent psychological needs of individuals, groups and organizations. CATSM, in a *facilitative attitudinal climate*, provides support and education, thus allowing the opportunity for discussion of the incident, an understanding of the many possible reactions, and information on how to manage stress associated with the event.

The core mission of CATSM is to establish connections between caregivers, individuals and groups of people who have been exposed to a traumatic event.

As a provider of human service, whether it is in emergency service, a medical or health-related service, clergy, catastrophe response, management or supervision, you are well trained to carry out your appointed tasks. And, you appreciate the dangers and problems that can occur if you ignore or deviate from accepted practice, protocol and procedures. In the face of traumatic exposure, it is also important that you are familiar with the emotional, cognitive, behavioral, physiological and spiritual reactions suggestive of traumatic stress. Moreover, it is critical that you understand the danger of ignoring these variables.

Regardless of the work that we do, or the role we play with the victims of a traumatic event, it is important that we address the "whole person," considering their physical, emotional, mental, social and spiritual needs. Only in this way can we effectively stabilize a crisis.

Similarly, at the organizational level, the effect of a traumatic event can drastically alter an organization's ability to function safely and productively. It is imperative that management, at all levels, understand the many variables present during and after a traumatic event. The organization's ability to function is dependant upon the ability of each staff member to come to work functioning safely and productively.

Unfortunately, there is little information describing the acute psychological reactions experienced by people *during* traumatic exposure. There is even less information available offering specific strategies to mitigate traumatic stress reactions during a traumatic event. These factors often leave you to use your best judgment. However, as you know, the unpredictability and volatility of a traumatic event may cloud or impair your judgment. Having a preconceived plan, a *Traumatic Stress Response Protocol*, makes good sense.

It is important to note that for those who work in the emergency services, medicine and healthcare fields, your priority will be the stabilization of illness and injury and, ultimately, the preservation of life. These efforts

MUST take priority over all interventions. The application of CATSM will raise your level of care beyond traditional emergency medical intervention. It will afford you the opportunity to provide emotional support during a time when acute physical and safety needs are being met.

Overall, CATSM offers practical intervention strategies for addressing the wide spectrum of traumatic experiences, from mild to the most severe, *during* traumatic events. It is delivered within the framework of a *facilitative or helping attitudinal climate* and aims to decrease the likelihood of acute traumatic stress reactions from becoming chronic stress disorders. CATSM is a goal-directed process aimed at "jump-starting" an individual's coping and problem-solving abilities. It seeks to stabilize acute symptoms of traumatic stress and stimulate healthy, adaptive functioning.

CATSM strives to *Prepare, Stabilize* and *Recover* individuals, groups and organizations following exposure to traumatic exposure.

In organizations, CATSM provides a framework to effectively manage traumatic events in three stages: **1. Pre-Incident Planning, 2. Engagement** and **3. Disengagement.** At its core, CATSM strives to *Prepare, Stabilize* and *Recover* individuals, groups and organizations following exposure to traumatic exposure.

Why does Comprehensive Acute Traumatic Stress Management utilize stages?

Having a preconceived plan, a series of logical and practical stages, will empower you to better address the complexity of individual, group and organizational needs *during* traumatic exposure. It will offer a degree of structure during a typically unstructured period of time, providing a solid framework for stabilizing the crisis situation. For example, while on catastrophe response duty in the wake of a tornado, an insurance company's CATSM Team member observed a young woman sitting on a refrigerator in the middle of a field. She was alone and in distress. As he approached her, he reviewed in his head the stages of the ATSM model: *Connect, Ground, Support, Normalize, Prepare.* Through this framework, he was able to approach, make a connection, and follow through with the stages. He commented later that just thinking through the model gave him a "road map," recalling that in the past, he would always avoid contact with victims unless it had to do solely with the claims process.

Any **reasonable step at mitigating a traumatic stress reaction is preferable to avoidance.**

ATSM was developed as a "stage model" to address the wide spectrum of traumatic experiences, from mild to the most severe. For example, the same fundamental stages that a Police Officer will follow when intervening with the victim of a burglary may be applied in intervention with family members who have just been informed of a loved one's death. The intensity of individual emotional, cognitive, behavioral, physiological and spiritual reactions will certainly vary during traumatic exposure. Consequently, appropriate intervention may not necessarily fall neatly into a linear progression of stages. Thus, you will need to be flexible given the presenting circumstances at hand.

How do you help someone when time is limited?

During a traumatic event, you may not have the time to progress through the stages of ATSM, and you will need to be flexible and adjust your expectations and goals. For example, you may have only a matter of seconds to recognize a potential acute traumatic stress reaction and to deliver one empathic, supportive statement (e.g., "I see that you're having a really tough time—I'll stay here with you."). In Chapter Three, practical information will be offered concerning the power of empathic communication. Remember, *any* reasonable step at mitigating a traumatic stress reaction is preferable to avoidance.

An example of the need for flexibility, while implementing the ATSM model when time is limited, is offered in the following example:

A call was received by 911 for a report of a partial building collapse. When units arrived on scene, they were confronted with a five-story building that had collapsed in the rear area during renovation. Construction workers informed the first arriving engine that at least two workers were missing. Search and rescue began. As search teams worked their way through debris, they heard a muffled cry from one of the workers. Within 1 hour and 20 minutes the crews were able to approach that trapped worker. As the first rescuer crawled into the location where the man was pinned, he immediately realized the victim was in acute emotional distress. He was conscious, panicking and only complained of pain in his left foot, which he could not free. The rescuer's first words to the victim were, "My name is Bob, I'm a firefighter. I've got you, I'm with you, I will not leave you. Now, I want you to take a deep breath and listen to me."

This example demonstrates the utilization of simple, straightforward statements to establish immediate connection, support and direction. As the minutes ticked by, this victim undoubtedly felt as though he was abandoned and alone. One can only imagine the thoughts that went through his mind during the time he had nothing to do but think. The nature of this rescue allowed little time for the provision of any comprehensive process. The victim required immediate assessment of life threat and brief psychological intervention to gain control while extrication proceeded.

Beyond time limitations, the applicability and efficacy of ATSM/CATSM will be influenced by several confounding variables. These factors will directly impact upon your ability to meet the emergent psychological needs of others (e.g., characteristics that are unique to the event, yourself, your profession, and those you serve).

Where does confidentiality fit in?

When addressing the emotional needs of others, you should make every effort to maintain confidentiality. Individuals' thoughts and feelings that are shared and entrusted with you, as well as identifying information, should remain in confidence. However, there are limits to confidentiality-particularly *during* a traumatic event. For example, information suggestive of medical conditions must be shared with medical personnel. Similarly, an individual who discloses self-destructive or homicidal ideation and/ or intent must be brought to the attention of both law enforcement and medical personnel. He will likely need further help. A child who reports that he has been abused should be brought to the attention of Child Protective Services. And finally, criminal behavior should be brought to the immediate attention of law enforcement officers. Your professional responsibilities, in concert with the nature of the event itself, will impact upon your ability to keep information in confidence.

CHAPTER THREE

The 10 Stages of Acute Traumatic Stress Management

This chapter focuses on the Acute Traumatic Stress Management (ATSM) model originally introduced as a *Traumatic Stress Response Protocol for all Emergency Responders* (Lerner and Shelton, 2001). The expansion of this model, Comprehensive Acute Traumatic Stress Management (CATSM), offers a *Traumatic Stress Response Protocol for All Caregivers*. CATSM, and its application with groups and organizations, will be addressed, in detail, in Chapter Five.

The ATSM process follows ten sequential stages. Each of these stages provides a framework for the management of emergent psychological needs *during* a traumatic event. The first four stages address immediate concerns regarding life threat and most often will be addressed by those charged with emergency care responsibilities. This group includes police officers, paramedics, firefighters, medical and nursing personnel. Overlooking interventions described in these initial stages may compromise your safety, the safety of others, and possibly lead to a failure in meeting the emergent, potentially life-saving needs of those you are called to serve. The following six stages are "traumatic stress specific." In addition to emergency response personnel, these stages may be applied by all caregivers who address emergent needs (e.g., organizational management, supervisory staff, clergy, claims industry catastrophe response teams, disaster response teams, educators, etc.). It is imperative that we always treat life threatening illness and injury prior to addressing psychological needs.

> **It is imperative that we always treat life threatening illness and injury prior to addressing psychological needs.**

Although ATSM was originally developed primarily for one-on-one intervention, it may certainly be applied with several individuals or with a small group of individuals. However, having more than one person implementing ATSM with only one victim may be perceived as threatening to a person who is feeling emotionally overwhelmed by the traumatic event itself.

1. Assess for Danger/Safety for Self and Others

Upon arrival at the scene of a traumatic event, it is crucial that you first assess the situation in order to determine whether there are any factors that can compromise your safety or the safety of others. You will be of little help to someone else if you are injured at the scene. Depending upon the nature of the event, it may be necessary to approach with police/security or other emergency personnel. It may be important to remove the individual(s) from a location, or from other individuals, rather than risk further traumatic exposure. For example, immediately after a serious automobile accident, a police officer asked an uninjured passenger who was seated in the back seat, and who had been evaluated by EMS, to "come and take a walk." The officer was cognizant of the fact that the front passenger was severely injured and that this young man was "loading" additional "traumatic baggage" (e.g., watching the "jaws of life" extricating his friend, hearing the sounds of the equipment, smelling the fumes, etc.). Similarly, a Catastrophe Response Team member on duty at the site of a major hurricane noted, while interviewing a client in front of his destroyed home, a "vacant stare" and "teary eyes" as they discussed the damage. The team member realized the victim was fixating on the remains of his home and all he had lost. He gently took the victim by the arm, turned him away from the vision of destruction, and began to slowly walk him away from the site.

2. Consider the Mechanism of Injury

Form an initial impression of the victim. In order to understand the nature of an individual's exposure to a traumatic event, it is important for you to assess how the event may have physically impacted the individual—that is, how environmental factors transferred to the person. For example, the type and extent of damage to the rear bumper of a vehicle may yield some insight into the nature of the victim's complaints of neck pain.

Having a physical injury may increase the likelihood of traumatic stress, as well as the potential for a posttraumatic stress disorder. For example, physical pain and discomfort are often cues that trigger feelings of anxiety, anger, depression, guilt, etc. Furthermore, the way in which an injury was sustained is important, and will influence this potential as well. For example, injuries that are sustained through an event of "intentional human design" (IHD), those that are "man-made" (e.g., a terrorist bombing or violent acts), have greater potential of causing a posttraumatic stress reaction than a naturally occurring event (e.g., a hurricane).

Similarly, injuries that are sustained through senseless actions may have a greater likelihood of causing traumatic stress. For example, the mother of a boy who lost his hand to a Fourth of July incident involving an M80 firecracker was particularly traumatized by the senseless cause of his life-altering injury.

When considering the mechanism of injury, and how environmental factors might have physically transferred to the person, it is also important to consider the *perceptual* experiences of victims. As indicated previously, particularly uncomfortable sights such as total destruction of homes from storms or fire, severe burns, dismemberment, open wounds and viewing the dead will leave a powerful impact on those who are directly involved with, or those who witness, the event. Similarly, the sounds of people screaming and the smell of deployed air bags will etch a lasting impression in the individual's psyche. Collectively, these may be called, the "Imprint of Horror." Remember, ATSM challenges you to address the needs of the "whole person," not just physical needs.

When considering the mechanism of injury, and how environmental factors might have physically transferred to the person, it is also important to consider the *perceptual* experiences of victims.

35

3. Evaluate the Level of Responsiveness

It is important for you to determine if an individual is alert and responsive to verbal stimuli. Does he feel pain? Is he aware of what has occurred, or what is presently occurring? Is he under the influence of a substance?

During a traumatic event it is quite possible that the individual is in "emotional" shock. Therefore, symptoms may mimic acute medical conditions (i.e., rapid changes in respiration, pulse, blood pressure, etc.). Recognize that a psychological state of shock may be adaptive in preventing the individual from experiencing the full impact of the event too quickly.

Exposure to traumatic events may precipitate the development of psychogenic shock (i.e., fainting). This form of shock may occur in the victim who has been exposed to a horrific event, causing the blood vessels to rapidly dilate resulting in a disruption of blood to the brain. Generally, this form of shock is self-correcting. Once the victim has fainted, the flow of blood increases to the brain and the shock state is remedied. It is important for anyone providing ATSM to recognize the signs and symptoms of shock, and to *immediately* obtain appropriate medical assistance. Look for the following signs and symptoms:

- Weakness
- Nausea with possible vomiting
- Increasing thirst
- Labored breathing
- Dizziness
- Restlessness
- Cool and clammy skin (may be profuse sweating) that has an ashen gray appearance
- Fear
- Altered mental status manifesting as disorientation, confusion, and unresponsiveness leading to unconsciousness.

Prevent fainting:

Have the victim sit down, lower their head between their knees. Prevent the victim from falling from this position. Do not use this technique for any victim with possible spinal injury, fracture or breathing difficulty.

If you are providing ATSM, and the signs and symptoms of shock develop, do the following:

- Immediately call for EMS.
- Have the victim lie down and stay at rest.
- Do not give the victim anything by mouth.
- If the victim has fainted and regained consciousness, do not allow him to stand.
- Properly position the victim:
    - *Elevate the lower extremities.* Place the victim flat, face up, and elevate the legs 8 – 12 inches. Do not elevate the legs if there is any suspicion of leg or pelvic fracture.
    - *Lay the victim flat, face up.* Use this position for victims with serious injuries to the extremities.
    - *Slightly raise head and shoulders when breathing difficulty is present.* Use this position only for conscious victims with **no possible neck, spinal, chest or abdominal injury**.

4. Address Medical Needs
Fire, Police, EMS, Medical/Nursing personnel

As an emergency responder, you have been trained to assess the ABCs (i.e., airway, breathing and circulation). You know that if an individual is not breathing, there will be little else that can be done to help him. You understand the importance of addressing significant signs and symptoms (e.g., severe chest pains) as well as the importance of knowing about existing medical conditions (e.g., diabetes). You have also been trained to know the kinds of injuries that may present a threat to life (e.g., internal bleeding). For all other emergency responders (i.e. catastrophe response teams, disaster recovery workers, clergy etc.) who are not specifically trained to manage acute medical conditions, you must yield this responsibility to those who are trained to do so. Once again, it is imperative that you always treat life threatening illness and injury prior to addressing emergent psychological needs.

5. Observe & Identify

This observation and identification stage may be viewed as the first "traumatic stress specific" stage. The primary objective during this early phase of intervention is to observe and identify those who have been exposed to the traumatic event. Very often, these individuals will not be the direct victims whom you have been called to serve. They may be "secondary" or "hidden victims." Remember, witnessing or being exposed to another individual who has faced traumatic exposure can cause traumatic stress. Consider the following examples:

A police officer responded to an aided call involving a middle-aged man who was reportedly in cardiac arrest. When he arrived, he found paramedics and other officers working on the man. As he walked through the living room of the home, he noticed a woman sitting in tears in a dark kitchen. He introduced himself to the man's wife and began to address her fear. She was indeed a candidate for ATSM, while her husband was not.

On prom night, for the local high school, a limo carrying 6 couples was involved in a serious accident, resulting in the death of 2 of the students and critically injuring 3 others. Word of the accident spread quickly and over 30 students and family members descended on the emergency room where the victims had been transported. The level of psychological distress in this group of friends and family was significant. While none of this group required medical management, all required psychological support. Utilizing the ATSM process, staff members addressed emergent psychological needs on an individual and group basis.

Following a plane crash, a group of boys from a youth naval organization was brought to the shore to observe search and rescue—as well as recovery efforts by the Coast Guard. The boys were actually being exposed to the movement of human remains. Fortunately, a member of the CATSM Team noticed the boys and asked that they be moved to another location. These boys were exposed to the "inner perimeter" of a highly traumatic event and could easily have become victimized themselves.

Upon arriving at a "routine call" for a car fire, a veteran firefighter determined that the driver had escaped physical injury. While his fellow firefighters fought the blaze, he observed the young driver standing nearby, with crossed arms. She appeared dazed and lost. When he approached her and asked whether she was okay, she said nothing and seemed to be "in her own world." This young woman was experiencing traumatic stress, and the firefighter was in an ideal position to begin addressing her emergent psychological needs.

As you observe and identify who has been exposed to a traumatic event (i.e., directly and/or indirectly), begin to observe and identify who is evidencing signs of traumatic stress. As emphasized previously, it is critical that you learn to recognize emotional, cognitive, behavioral, physiological and spiritual reactions suggestive of traumatic stress (see specific traumatic stress reactions delineated in Chapter One and summarized in the Appendices). Carefully look around you. Anyone, including yourself, may be a direct or hidden victim.

Finally, as an emergency responder, catastrophe response team member, clergy, or disaster worker, your professional responsibilities will often necessitate direct involvement in the "inner perimeter" of tragedies. This exposure will increase the likelihood that *you* will experience traumatic stress. If a sufficient number of personnel are managing the requisite tasks in the inner perimeter, and your direct involvement is not necessary, give thought to remaining outside the inner perimeter. Consider the following example:

At the scene of a major building collapse, many victims had died. Much of the death was gruesome, as a result of the forces involved. Initial responding police, fire and EMS were confronted with very difficult sights as they attempted rescue and, eventually, body recovery. As disaster services arrived on scene in the hours and days following the tragedy, this group of secondary responders were also exposed to the horrific sights still present. Psychological support services were established in the outer perimeter in order to address the emotional needs of the workers. Personnel trained in ATSM were available in the inner perimeter to provide immediate psychological support to distressed workers. In addition, personnel were limited in the time they spent in the inner perimeter, and non-essential personnel were denied entry to lessen overall staff exposure.

Police officers, paramedics and firefighters were called to an automobile accident in which a vehicle reportedly left the highway and crashed in the woods. When these responders arrived, they observed a nearly decapitated teenage girl, who had been ejected from the vehicle, impaled on a tree. The horrific sight took its toll on even the most seasoned professionals. One of the police officers who arrived at the scene elected to not approach and, instead, remained out of the inner perimeter. Familiar with ATSM, he offered support for those who had been directly exposed to the gruesome scene.

Remember, a percentage of people who you are called to help will require immediate safety and/or life saving measures. They are not candidates for ATSM.

As an emergency responder, you will be more effective in addressing the emergent psychological needs of others if you have not been exposed to the intensity of the event yourself. Clearly, your decision to remain out of the inner perimeter must take into consideration that you are in no way compromising the safety and well-being of others.

6. Connect with the Individual

This stage should only begin after you (or another qualified person) have addressed the previous stages. Once you have identified an individual with whom you will work, you should introduce yourself and state your title and/or position. For example, following a tornado a member of the clergy from a neighboring community responded to provide whatever support he could. He was not dressed in a manner that would identify him as clergy. While walking through the debris field he came upon a young man who was wandering aimlessly, searching for members of his family. He approached the man and stated "Hi, I'm Father Bob from Holy Name Church in Westdale and your name is?" If you know the person's name— use it. This simple, direct statement establishes a connection and may be accompanied by an extension of your hand.

If you have not already done so, and he *has* been medically evaluated, attempt to move the individual away from the stressor, as previously described. Try to prevent further traumatic exposure by utilizing a diversionary tactic (e.g., "Come, let's take a walk...."). If this is not possible, position yourself so the individual is not looking directly at the scene. During this early phase of intervention, your mission is to begin to lessen traumatic stress exposure. Presenting a different scene will help accomplish this goal.

Victims exposed to traumatic events can present a wide range of emotional, cognitive, behavioral, physiological and spiritual reactions. Some of these reactions are predictable, some are not. At all times you must be aware of your safety. Do the following:

- When approaching the victim remain in a ***protective stance***. Approach with your strong side forward, weight on your strong leg, prepared to spring back, away from a potentially violent reaction. Never stand flatfooted directly facing the victim. This position will allow you no ability to move quickly out of harms way.

- Create a ***reactionary gap***. The reactionary gap allows space between you and the victim and is necessary while you are making your initial impression (cautionary approach). This gap should be between 6-8 feet. As you determine no threat exists, you may close this gap and proceed with the *connecting phase* of ATSM.

- Place yourself in the ***position of advantage.*** The position of advantage provides you with an escape route should it be needed. Ask yourself, "If I need to get away quickly, is the door at my back or the victims back blocking me in? Does the debris block my ability to move quickly to a place of safety?" The more confined the space, the greater the need for you to consider your escape route.

Awareness of these three points will help ensure your safety while working with potentially unstable individuals. Truly an ounce of prevention is worth a pound of cure.

Next, begin to develop rapport by making an effort to understand and appreciate his situation. A simple question such as, "How are you doing?" may be used to engage the individual. Once again, try to use his name when you speak with him. If possible, have him sit down and sit down with him. Attempt to make eye contact and turn your body toward him.

Try to touch his shoulder if it feels right or even hold his hand. Speak with him in a calm, supportive tone. These actions may help you to be perceived as warm and genuine. Characteristics of the person, the nature of the event, etc. will influence your approach. For example, an intoxicated individual or someone who has sustained a head injury may be agitated and combative. Getting too close, at eye level, or making physical contact may cause the individual to strikeout at you. Similarly, making physical contact with someone who has just been raped may not be constructive and may cause the victim to withdraw. Overall, "connecting" should be viewed as an ongoing process in ATSM.

During this age of information and technology, we can communicate from nearly anywhere at nearly any given time. The advent of pagers and cell phones may be very helpful tools for reaching others. For example, offering a young victim of an automobile accident the ability to contact her parents may bolster your connection with the young woman. Certainly, there will be a risk in not knowing how helpful the receiving party will ultimately be. Recognize also that this ability to rapidly communicate can significantly interfere with your responsibilities as an emergency responder. Consider the following example:

> A 22 year-old man was killed while riding his motorcycle just blocks from his parents' home. A passerby recognized his mangled bike and used her cell phone to contact the young man's parents. Within minutes, police found themselves wrestling with a highly distraught mother and father who exposed themselves to a horrific accident scene involving their son. This compromised the police officers' ability to preserve and investigate the scene and further traumatized bystanders and the emergency responders.

"Connecting" should be viewed as an ongoing process in ATSM.

What specific strategies may be utilized to connect with particularly challenging, emotionally distraught, individuals?

During traumatic exposure, individual reactions may present on a continuum from a totally detached, withdrawn reaction to the most intense displays of emotion (e.g., uncontrollable crying, screaming, panic, anger, fear, etc.). These situations present a considerable challenge. In order to address an individual's emergent psychological needs, you must "break through" these emotional states.

As described previously, be sure to address the initial stages of ATSM (i.e., emergency medical protocol) prior to attempts at connecting with the challenging individual. Following, are five highly practical techniques that you may utilize to engage these individuals. These strategies may be referred to as the "Five D's"—1) Distraction, 2) Disruption, 3) Diffusion. 4) Decision, and 5) Direction.

1. Distraction

This technique aims to distract and refocus the challenging individual. The approach may be likened to a strategy that is often used by parents of young children. When the child shows interest in the TV remote control, the parent distracts the child with a "transitional object"—a more appropriate, yet interesting toy. In the same way, when an individual is unresponsive to efforts to engage, or possibly at the other end of the continuum crying uncontrollably, you may distract and refocus the individual. Introduce an irrelevant ,yet highly interesting topic. The more concise and thought-provoking the topic is, the better. Consider the following example:

An emergency medical service supervisor raced to the scene of a child who was reportedly choking. When he arrived at the scene, a paramedic was walking the girl out the front door of a home toward the waiting ambulance. The medic reported to his supervisor that the child had a small piece of chicken bone lodged in her soft pallet. The child was teary-eyed and coughing gently—as if to clear her throat. Following the child out the door were a number of young siblings and family friends. They were crying uncontrollably and seemed to be "feeding off" each other's level of hysteria. The EMS supervisor walked over to the children and said, "I feel so sorry for you guys!" He immediately caught their attention. He then followed with, "You're all going to have to go to your piggy banks to get some money to buy ice cream for your friend—she's going to have a sore throat when she comes home later." The children's reactions quickly, almost magically, shifted to laughing. Having the kids engaged, he then lowered himself to one knee and gave them a chance to "tell their story" of how scary it was seeing their friend choking and to review the facts of the event. Following the ATSM model, he then supported them, normalized their reactions and prepared them for her return home.

The key to this Distraction Technique is that the topic that is introduced, or the comment that is made, is sufficiently powerful to distract and divert the individual's attention. Be careful not to say something that implies a lack of concern. Also, make sure that you subsequently return to the reality of the situation by discussing the event at a factual level.

2. Disruption

A second strategy that may be utilized with challenging individuals involves a powerful disruption of the emotional reaction. First, come down to the person's level, either kneeling or sitting, and establish eye contact. In a clear and calm voice, while looking directly into the individual's eyes,

Perhaps the greatest advantage of this *Disruption Technique* is that it can be implemented very quickly.

give a basic command using his/her name: "Mary, I want you to take a deep breath." Then pause, and in a slightly louder more forceful voice, repeat the command exactly as stated: "Mary, I want you to take a deep breath." Continue to repeat the command, always using the same words. Escalate the volume and tone with each command statement. Usually, by the third command the individual will follow your request. At this moment, lower your voice to a calm level and begin to talk. You may instruct the individual to take a second and third slow deep breath. Once you have broken through the emotional state, you will be able to provide direction and support.

Perhaps the greatest advantage of this *Disruption Technique* is that it can be implemented very quickly. Recognize that by utilizing the technique, you will likely be doing something very different from others. For example, your focus on the individual's breathing may disrupt a seemingly ineffective cycle of effort, by others, to gain control over hysterical behavior.

3. Diffusion

A third strategy for connecting with the challenging individual involves diffusion of the emotional state. For example, you may begin your conversation with an anxious or possibly agitated individual at a voice rate and tone comparable to his. If he is speaking loudly, increase your volume to match his. If he is speaking rapidly, speak rapidly. If you are required to move around with the individual, match his pace. Gradually, begin to slow the physical pace, lower the volume of your voice and slow your rate of speech. As the individual begins to respond in a calm, more controlled manner, provide direction and support. Move him away from the scene, have him take a deep breath and continue with the ATSM process.

Interestingly, this technique may also be utilized in the opposite direction. For example, with a seemingly depressed or generally non-communicative individual, begin your conversation with the individual at a voice rate and tone comparable to his. If he is speaking softly, decrease your volume to match his. If he is speaking slowly, speak slowly. If you are required to move around with the individual, match his pace. Gradually, begin to increase the physical pace, raise the volume of your voice and increase your rate of speech. As the individual begins to respond in a more energetic, involved manner, provide direction and support. Move him away from the scene, have him take a deep breath and continue with the ATSM process.

4. Decision

A fourth strategy, often effective in dealing with a challenging individual, involves having the victim make a decision. Being asked to decide between two basic choices often distracts the challenging individual and focuses him on adaptive, constructive behavior. It gives an individual who is feeling out-of-control during a crisis the ability to regain a sense of control through his decision-making. Consider the following:

> *After learning that her co-worker had suffered a sudden heart attack and died the night before, a young employee, Jennifer, sat at her desk crying hysterically. She was inconsolable. When Jennifer was asked if she would like to take a walk to the ladies lounge on the South side of the third floor, or sit in the atrium under the new palm trees, she chose the latter. This decision, involving some detailed choices, diverted Jennifer's attention and "short-circuited" her thinking. Once in the atrium, efforts to connect with Jennifer were more effective.*

5. Direction

As indicated previously, particularly when time is limited, providing clear authoritative direction is often an effective vehicle for gaining rapid control. The challenging individual who remains non-responsive to a warm and supportive effort to connect may respond to firm direction. Consider this example:

> *After hearing reports of a teenage boy disappearing under a wave while buggy-boarding, lifeguards found themselves wrestling with two agitated boys who were racing into the ocean to find him. A strong undertow was compromising their safety. A senior lifeguard called for immediate assistance. One lifeguard remained with the boys, speaking calmly with them—trying to engage them. This approach only seemed to escalate the boys' agitation and even, rage. A park police officer arrived at the scene, sized-up the event, and immediately directed the boys in a loud, stern voice to, "take a seat" on their boards. In this case, the police officer was able to gain rapid control and begin a constructive process of fact-finding by utilizing authoritative direction.*

When considering the utilization of *Distraction, Disruption, Diffusion, Decision* or *Direction*, realize that the nature of the event, time variables and individuals' responses will influence your approach. For example, the Diffusion technique, by its very nature, will take more time to implement than the Distraction, Disruption, Decision or Direction techniques. Notwithstanding, it may be the best choice given a particular situation.

The "Five D's" are practical intervention techniques. However, they *must* be practiced. Breaking through strong emotional reactions *during* a traumatic event will require a confident, well-rehearsed approach. Having strong familiarity with these strategies will enable you to apply them with the most challenging individuals.

7. Ground the Individual

When you have established a connection with an individual who has been exposed to a traumatic event (e.g., eye contact, body turned toward you, dialogue directed at you, etc.), you can initiate this grounding stage. Begin by acknowledging the traumatic event at a *factual* level. Here, you attempt to orient the individual by discussing the facts surrounding the event. For example, while working with a gunshot victim, an emergency room nurse might say, "You were involved in a shooting. A bullet entered your right side, and we are working to control bleeding inside your body."

During this important phase, we try to address the circumstances surrounding the event at a cognitive, or thinking level. While we do not discourage the expression of emotion, we attempt to focus on the facts in the here-and-now, and help the individual to know the reality of the situation. Oftentimes, his "reality" may be seriously clouded due to the nature of the event. Remember, traumatic events overwhelm an individual's usual coping and problem-solving abilities. Assure the individual that he is now safe, if he is.

By reviewing facts, you may disrupt "negative cognitive rehearsal" and help the individual to begin to deal with the actual circumstances at hand. In other words, the individual may still be "playing the tape" of the accident over and over in her head. For example, after being extricated from a car that was on fire, two young women were sitting on the side of the road in tears. When asked how they were doing, one responded, "I can't get out!" Cognitively, she was "still in" the vehicle.

> **During this important phase, we try to address the circumstances surrounding the event at a cognitive, or thinking level.**

It is important to "place the individual in the situation." Encourage him to "tell his story" and describe where he was, what he saw, what it sounded like, what it smelled like, what he did, and how his body responded. Encourage the individual to discuss his behavioral and physiological response to the event-rather than how it felt.

As indicated previously, you should not discourage the expression of emotion. Rather, your aim here is to attempt to focus the individual on the facts surrounding the event itself and his behavioral and physiological responses to the event.

What can I say if I find myself at a loss for words?

This is a common experience for all people who try to help others who are struggling with painful thoughts and feelings. Human nature often pushes us to try to make people feel better quickly. Hence, too often caregivers become advice givers. Do not become an expert in solving another person's problem. Instead, become an expert in helping another person to find the strength within himself to make adaptive, healthy decisions.

 If you find yourself at a loss for words and you are experiencing a great deal of "dead air," try sticking with the facts (e.g., "Which vehicle struck the back of the trailer first?") or ("What were you doing when the storm hit?"), his behaviors (i.e., "What exactly did you do after you heard the sound of the impact, the wind, rain, etc.?") and his physiological response (e.g., "What did the air bag feel like when it deployed?" "What happened when the house began to shake?" "What did you hear?"). In all likelihood, talking about facts, as well as the individual's behavioral and physiological response, will stimulate thoughts and feelings. This movement will prompt you to initiate the next "support" phase.

Before leaving this section on grounding, once again, remember that the characteristics of the person, the nature of the event, etc. will influence your approach. For example, a young child may be unable to "tell his story" or even begin to understand what has occurred. Any efforts to "ground him," and to discuss facts surrounding the event, must be made consistent with his developmental level. In the face of traumatic exposure, a young child may likely regress and only be concerned that he will be abandoned. Therefore, moving quickly to a supportive mode makes good sense.

8. Provide Support

Factual discussion and the realization of a traumatic event, particularly when the event is still occurring, may likely stimulate thoughts and feelings. This is often the time when individuals who are exposed to trauma need the most support. However, in reality, it is also the time when many people look the other way—including emergency responders. Many people feel terribly unprepared to handle other individuals' painful thoughts and feelings. Oftentimes, they fear that they will "open a can of worms" or "say the wrong thing." This section is aimed at providing a practical strategy to address thoughts and feelings.

The establishment of a *facilitative or helping attitudinal climate* is perhaps most critical during this supportive stage. In this climate, you attempt to understand and respect the uniqueness of the individual—the thoughts and feelings that he is experiencing. You strive to "give back" a sense of control that has been "taken from" him by virtue of his exposure to the event. You support him, and you allow him to think and feel.

In the face of traumatic exposure, many people experience an overwhelming sense of aloneness and withdraw into their own world. You should make a respectful effort to "enter that world," and to help the individual to know that he is not alone and that his unique perception of his experience is important. Do not attempt to talk a person out of a feeling (e.g., "Don't be scared, you're fine.").

Are there specific guidelines to know what is okay to say?

There are no "cookbook" approaches to supporting an individual during a traumatic event. However, by operating within the framework of a facilitative attitudinal climate, you will more likely say and do things that will lead to a healthy, adaptive adjustment in those you serve. For example, you would encourage an individual to express his feelings of anger, sadness, grief, guilt, etc. Most importantly, you would respect an individuals' unique perception of his experience.

When you are empathic with those you are called to serve, you realize, understand and communicate an appreciation of the other person's experience.

Within the framework of this attitudinal climate, you will refrain from saying and doing things that would likely lead to an unhealthy, maladaptive adjustment. For example, you would not be confrontational or challenging with an individual who felt differently about a situation than you, and you would not dismiss another person's fears by saying, "Everything is going to be okay...." at a time when everything was not okay for him.

How can I deal with peoples' feelings and still get the job done?

There is a crucial mechanism that will enable you to address the emotional needs of others, while keeping yourself grounded and functional during a traumatic event. It is perhaps the single most important ingredient in establishing a facilitative or helping attitudinal climate—*empathy*.

When you are empathic with those you are called to serve, you realize, understand and communicate an appreciation of the other person's experience. You attempt to understand the feelings that lie behind his words (or perhaps actions) and convey that understanding to him.

It is important that empathy not be confused with sympathy. Someone who becomes sympathetic begins to feel sorry for another person. If you become sympathetic, you will likely become a part of the problem and fall prey to becoming "secondarily victimized" yourself. You will invest considerable energy experiencing another person's pain and suffering. You will no longer remain grounded and functional, and your decision-making abilities will likely become clouded. As an empathic responder however, you will only invest energy in realizing, understanding and communicating an appreciation for another person's pain and suffering.

How can I become more empathic?

Unlike other characteristics of effective counselors and caregivers (e.g., warmth and genuineness), empathy is rather easily taught and learned. As a provider of ATSM, you should work at developing and enhancing your empathic listening skills.

By actively listening, you will find yourself attending to important details—including the feelings that lie behind the words. Then, you may begin to "test" your understanding of the other person's experience. For example, when your statements to others are met with affirmative responses such as, "Right," "Yeah" or "Exactly," you will have a strong indication that you are communicating empathically and that the other person feels understood—that you truly hear him and that you are with him.

The following are examples of empathic responses/statements:

- "You seem scared and alone right now."

- "It's like you just can't stop playing the tape of the accident over and over in your head."

- "It sounds like you've been through a tough time."

- "Help me understand what you're thinking. It seems like you're frustrated with us."

- "I see that you're having difficulty concentrating right now."

- "Listening to you, it seems as though you're angry at the officer because you felt that he sided with the other driver."

- "If I'm hearing you correctly, it sounds like the pain is primarily in your right shoulder."

- "I can see that you're doing a lot of thinking."

- "So, you feel that you were treated disrespectfully."

The scientific literature concerning intervention with survivors of traumatic events consistently supports the notion of exposing individuals to their thoughts and feelings surrounding the event. Such exposure may serve to counter dissociative feelings (i.e., feelings of detachment) that often emerge through traumatic exposure.

Empathic communication, within the framework of a supportive attitudinal climate, may likely facilitate early expression and expose an individual to his overwhelming thoughts and feelings. This kind of exposure may catapult an individual into an adaptive, problem-solving mode.

How may empathy be utilized with a potentially self-destructive individual?

Empathy may serve to ease painful feelings of aloneness that are often associated with traumatic exposure. One particularly difficult experience for all ATSM providers, one that truly underscores the most acute feelings of aloneness experienced by a person, is intervention with a self-destructive or suicidal individual. Consider the following examples:

> *After the loss of his home and two dogs resulting from a wild fire that had burned thousands of acres, a young man said to his wife, "I can't take anymore of this, I've lost it all, I just want to be dead." At that point, he took his shotgun and walked away from a burned-out structure that used to be home. His wife was in a state of panic and unable to stop him. She ran from the house in search of anyone who could help her.*
>
> *The first person she found was a disaster relief worker who was surveying damage. She told him what had just occurred and he immediately began to search for her husband. Within 10 minutes he found him—sitting in a burned ravine, holding the shotgun at his side. Concerned for his*

safety, the worker approached slowly and was eventually able to sit down next to the man. Conversation began and the husband stated, "I'm done, this is the last straw, I'll never be able to recover from this, she will do well with my insurance money, I'm worth more dead than alive." The worker commented, "Don't say you're done. You're not done, this can all be rebuilt, you have a wife and a kid to live for. It could have been a lot worse—you could have lost them too." The husband turned away from the relief worker and asked to be left alone.

After a lengthy argument, a young man said good-bye to his wife and told her that he wouldn't be around anymore. He went into their garage, locked the door and started the car's engine. After several minutes, his wife thought to check on him. She was able to get into the garage and turn the engine off. Her husband appeared to be semiconscious. She immediately called 911. Within minutes, police officers arrived and found the young man sitting in a chair in his backyard smoking a cigarette. His eyes were very red. He told the officers that his wife didn't appreciate him, that he had no reason to live, that he was 'fine' and wanted to be left alone. One of the officers explained to the young man that he made a "stupid decision," that he was lucky to be alive, lucky to have such a pretty wife, and lucky to have such a beautiful home. The man repeatedly asked to be left alone and said that everything was hopeless.

> The pain of being misunderstood is possibly greater than the pain of being left completely alone!

In both of these examples, there was no effort to realize, understand or convey any appreciation for the circumstance. In fact, the pain of being misunderstood was possibly greater than the pain of being left completely alone!

How helpful would it have been for the disaster worker or police officer to begin to establish a facilitative attitudinal climate? What would have happened if they had said something like, "I see you've been through one hell of a night. I'm glad that I can be here for you now." Would these men have been fixed? Would they no longer have wanted to harm themselves?

In all likelihood, they would hardly have been "fixed" and no longer have any thoughts of ending their life. However, they might have begun to feel a sense of being understood that was apparently so lacking in their existence—a feeling of aloneness, hopelessness and desperation that led them to want to kill themselves. By establishing a facilitative attitudinal climate, the disaster worker and police officer might have begun a helping and healing process. They might have opened the door to a level of appreciation for these men that they were "not alone" in the world and that help may be out there. Furthermore, they may have set the stage for hospital personnel or mental health professionals by generating a level of receptivity for help.

A facilitative attitudinal climate is a necessary, and oftentimes sufficient, component in supporting an individual and in mitigating acute traumatic stress reactions during traumatic exposure. Intervention, without this attitudinal climate, may likely be perceived as a cold technique.

Finally, it may be helpful to introduce some basic anxiety management techniques such as asking the individual to take a slow deep breath through his nose and then slowly exhale through his mouth. Recognize that the implementation of more specific strategies or skills (e.g., progressive muscle relaxation, cognitive restructuring, hypnosis, etc.) should only be implemented by individuals who have been properly trained to do so.

9. Normalize the Response

While you are attempting to support an individual by giving him the opportunity to express his thoughts and feelings, begin to normalize his reaction to the traumatic event. This is an important component when intervening with people who have been exposed to trauma and may be feeling very alone. Experiencing a cascade of emotions, or perhaps a lack of emotional expression, may cause him to feel as if he is "losing it" and perhaps, "going crazy."

Normalizing and validating an individual's experience will help him to know that he is a normal person trying to deal with an abnormal event. It is important that you do not become sympathetic and over identify with the situation with statements such as, "I know what it feels like... a close friend of mine was killed in a car accident last year." Rather, you should attempt to normalize and validate the individual's experience with statements like, "I see this is overwhelming for you right now... This kind of experience would be hard for anyone to handle."

Another important component of the normalization process is to begin to educate the individual by helping him to know how people typically respond to trauma. Consider the following example:

> *While interviewing a victim who was assaulted in a failed car-jacking attempt, a police officer recognized that the man was experiencing an acute traumatic stress reaction. The man sustained only a small laceration on his right forearm. However, he was very anxious and seemed to vacillate between intense feelings of fear and anger. He was perspiring heavily, his legs were shaking, he said that he couldn't stop thinking about the perpetrator and that nothing seemed real—like he was watching himself in a movie.*
>
> *After moving through a process of connecting and then grounding the man with facts, the officer began to support him by showing an understanding and an appreciation for his feelings (e.g., "You seem scared and angry, and it's hard for you believe this whole thing is over."). The officer began to normalize the man's experience (e.g., "This kind of thing would cause just about anyone to be fearful and ticked-off."). Then, the officer educated him about the nature of traumatic stress. He explained that when people are exposed to traumatic events it is normal for them to feel the kinds of things he was experiencing.*

Normalizing and validating an individual's experience will help him to know that he is a normal person trying to deal with an abnormal event.

Like any other active intervention, educating an individual who has been exposed to a traumatic event will be influenced by many factors.

The "Validation Technique" is often helpful in normalizing an individual's experience. It has three components.

1) Recognize the person's response to the traumatic event.
2) Tie a validating statement to the individual's response.
3) Immediately explain, at a factual level, why you have come to that conclusion.

For example, in the situation above, the police officer could have (1) recognized that the man was feeling shaky and overwhelmed. He then could have (2) tied a validating statement to the response by saying, "You should be feeling scared and angry." Then, he could have immediately (3) explained, at a factual level, why he came to that conclusion. "When someone hops in your car with a knife, tries to push you out, and you struggle and throw him out, it's pretty normal for you to feel scared and angry." Finally, the officer could conclude by saying, "You've been through a lot and you're responding like a normal person trying to cope with very negative, frightening experience!"

This technique is most effective with an individual who is showing some signs of adaptive or healthy coping. In this case, the gentleman was able to articulate his thoughts and feelings, and he seemed receptive to the officer's effort to help. This technique helps the individual to know that his experience is normal given the circumstances.

In the event that an individual did not evidence signs of healthy coping (e.g., if he appeared to be intoxicated, highly agitated and combative, extremely emotional, catatonic, hypervigilant, psychotic, etc.) then this technique would be inappropriate and possibly dangerous.

Overall, the primary purpose of the normalization stage is to help an individual who is experiencing traumatic stress to know that he is not alone, that he is a normal person trying to cope with an abnormal event—that his experience is perhaps his mind's attempt to "make sense of the senseless."

10. Prepare for the Future

The final phase of the ATSM process is aimed at preparing the individual for what lies on the road ahead. It is helpful to 1) review the nature of the traumatic event, 2) bring the person to the present, and 3) describe likely events in the future. The educational process initiated during the previous normalization stage will continue during this final stage of the ATSM process. Consider the following example:

After addressing medical needs, initiating a connection and beginning a grounding process with a 12 year-old boy who was struck by a car while riding his bicycle, a paramedic moved the youngster to a waiting ambulance. While in the ambulance, the medic supported the boy while he "told his story," describing his pain as well as his feelings of fear. The medic then gradually began to normalize the boy's experience by suggesting that it would be painful and scary for almost anyone.

After a short time, the medic began to prepare him for the future. He reiterated to the boy that because he was struck by a car and that his leg and shoulder were injured, doctors in the hospital emergency room would examine him. He explained that x-rays would help the doctors to know how to repair his injuries. The medic told the boy that his parents would probably meet him in the ER.

Finally, the medic explained to the youngster that he had been through a painful and scary experience and that he may find himself thinking about the accident over and over in his mind. He told the boy that this was very common and that, with time, it would be easier for him to handle. He also explained to the boy that he might find himself being a bit jumpy, and having some difficulty sleeping and that this was very normal too. Finally, the medic encouraged the boy to talk about the accident with his parents and to ask to speak with a counselor if he felt the need.

This preparation phase of the ATSM process is highly effective for all ATSM providers. Regardless of your role in the incident, emergency responder, catastrophe response team member, clergy, disaster relief worker or management/supervisory personnel, preparing people for the unknown will lessen distress. Remember, you know what will unfold in the next few hours, days and weeks based on your knowledge, experience and training. By sharing this information and educating the individual, you empower them to move forward with less fear.

When preparing an individual for the future, always be honest, do not offer information that may be misleading or is untrue. Acknowledge when you do not know. Offer to find answers to questions, if you can, and never make promises that you cannot keep.

Be careful not to tell someone as you near the end of your intervention that "everything is going to be okay" or that "everything is going to work out." As indicated previously, these kinds of "band-aid" statements may only serve to minimize an individual's feelings and cause him to feel misunderstood. Instead, focus on the facilitative attitudinal climate that you have established—"I'm glad that I had the opportunity to be here with you during such a difficult time."

Finally, encourage people to pursue further help, if need be, and provide appropriate referrals. Inform them of the existence of agencies that may be of assistance to them (e.g., community counseling centers, the Red Cross, etc.). Address every individual's concerns realistically and prepare them for a future in which they will ultimately exercise healthy, adaptive coping strategies.

Before leaving this description concerning the final stage of ATSM, remember to address your own thoughts and feelings. Take the time to speak with a peer in order to discuss your thoughts and reactions following the provision of ATSM. In doing so, you will lessen the likelihood that you will become victimized by the very event that you have been called to manage.

CHAPTER FOUR

Factors that Impact the Implementation of ATSM

The applicability and efficacy of ATSM may be influenced by a number of critical factors. These include: 1) characteristics that are unique to the caregiver's profession (e.g., police, fire, EMS, hospital emergency personnel, clergy, business management, human resources, EAP personnel, etc.), 2) characteristics of the caregiver, 3) characteristics of the individuals who are served, and 4) characteristics of the traumatic event. This section will explore the impact of each of these characteristics on the ATSM process.

1. Characteristics of Emergency Responders

The ATSM model is based upon the belief that early intervention, particularly *during* a traumatic event, can ultimately prevent acute difficulties from becoming chronic problems. Therefore, the model offers great utility for all emergency responders. However, it is important to understand that the specific discipline, as well as the "culture" of the responder's profession, may influence whether a helping attitudinal climate can or should be established. Additionally, the emergency responder's profession may directly influence the applicability of the ATSM stages. The following examples address this point.

> *An elderly woman clutched the shoulder of a firefighter who had carried her from her smoke-filled apartment. Once outside the building, the woman tried to engage the fireman in a discussion about her grandson who was injured fighting fires himself. The firefighter quickly abandoned the woman—she perceived him to be cold and distant. Several minutes later he saved another elderly resident from the burning building.*

Here, the **firefighter's** primary responsibility was to secure the safety of the residents during a fire. Efforts to address this woman's psychological needs were clearly secondary to the physical and safety needs of the residents in the building.

> *A paramedic arrived at the scene of an MVA. A middle-aged man who was reportedly resting his arm outside an open window, lost his arm after a truck broad-sided the vehicle. Although conscious and responsive, the man was bleeding profusely. While on the way to the medical center, the paramedic worked to control the bleeding and attended to the severed appendage that was packed in ice. The medic focused little attention on the man's fears and concerned himself with the emergent physical needs of the victim.*

The **paramedic's** primary objective was to address the man's acute physical and safety needs. While focusing on these needs, perhaps another emergency responder could have addressed the man's fears through ATSM.

> *A man who was suspected of sexually molesting an 8 year-old boy was caught and arrested by police. While in custody, he complained of chest pains, the "sweats," tightening of his jaw, and a shooting pain down his left arm. He was brought by police ambulance to the hospital. In the emergency room, the man appeared highly anxious and began to disclose to a nurse that he had indeed molested the child. The nurse did not acknowledge the man's statements and instead, focused on addressing his physical condition. Following the provision of emergent medical care, the nurse brought the man's statements to the attention of law enforcement personnel.*

In this case, the man's confession to the **nurse** was significant. However, the man's symptomatology was more significant and required immediate evaluation. The man was experiencing a heart attack.

Police officers are often the first responders at the scene of traumatic events. This places them in an ideal position to address emergent psychological needs during traumatic exposure—particularly for aided calls (i.e., when someone is sick or injured). However, the nature of the situation, in concert with a police officer's responsibilities, will dictate the appropriateness of addressing psychological variables. For example, when criminal activity is suspected, an investigative interview may be more appropriate than a progression through the stages of ATSM. However, it should be noted that addressing traumatic stress with empathy, even during a criminal interview, may facilitate the investigative process. For example, a police officer who recognized the emotional impact of his involvement when questioning a teenage shoplifter, initially responded empathically to the adolescent, "I understand that you're very scared right now. However,....." The teenager then cooperated with the officer and admitted taking the item from the store.

The unique responsibilities inherent in the emergency responder's profession will impact directly upon the applicability and efficacy of ATSM. Characteristics specific to the caregiver himself will be addressed in the next section.

2. Characteristics of the Caregiver

In providing emergency care to effectively address an individual's safety and acute medical needs, your approach is generally quite active and requires that you "take control of the scene." This fares well for the typical action-oriented emergency responder who enters the profession with a strong personality and a "need for control." Yet here lies a potential conflict.... When addressing psychological reactions and supporting an individual who has been exposed to a traumatic event, you must strive to "give back" a sense of control that has been "taken from" the individual by virtue of his exposure to the event. It will take a strong personality to be able to relinquish this control.

Much has been written about the seemingly detached posture that is exhibited by some emergency services personnel. This detachment has adaptive qualities. It protects you from becoming "a part of the problem" and enables you to "get the job done." However, there are certainly opportunities when safety and acute medical needs are not being addressed that you may attempt to meet the emergent psychological needs of those you serve. There is an opportunity to raise the level of care beyond traditional emergency medical intervention.

Like in all professions, there are many personalities represented in the emergency services. Consider the following example:

A police supervisor, a Sergeant, responded to a multi-vehicle automobile accident. When he arrived at the scene, fire department EMTs were moving boarded victims to several waiting ambulances and police officers were working to control traffic and speaking with witnesses. The Sergeant noticed a young boy, about 10 years of age, sitting on a guide rail with a bandaged arm and leg. He approached the child, introduced himself, got down in a catcher's squat, and moved through the stages of ATSM (i.e., connecting, grounding, supporting, normalizing, and preparing for the future).

Later in the evening when the streets quieted down, the Sergeant mentioned to his partner that he had to stop at the hospital to check on his buddy. His partner wondered which cop was laid-up in the hospital. The Sergeant walked-through the ER and came upon the young boy from the accident. He walked over toward the child and asked, "How's my buddy?" He gave the boy a 'high five' and said, "Just want you to know I'm thinkin' about you, pal." The parents of the child, with tears in their eyes, thanked him for coming. The father of the boy was overheard by a nurse saying softly to his wife, "This guy is one special cop; they should all be like him."

Just after leaving the hospital, the Sergeant in this vignette quickly shifted gears and responded to a call for a domestic disturbance. He did not mention the visit throughout the rest of the evening. His decision to visit the young boy in the hospital was personal and a reflection of his character.

3. Characteristics of the Individuals Whom You Serve

There will be factors, specific to the individuals with whom you intervene that may influence, interfere with or compromise your ability to implement the ATSM model (e.g., alcohol/substance involvement, violent individuals, sexual assault victims, the mentally challenged, young children, etc.).

This section will offer practical information, as well as some general guidelines, for managing these potentially confounding factors. This information is not intended to serve as a comprehensive model for addressing every type of individual's needs. Rather, it aims to provide some practical information that may be utilized in concert with the principles of ATSM. First, consider the following example. It brings several of these variables to light.

A paramedic was called to respond to an unconscious male in a store. When she arrived at the scene, she observed a middle-aged man standing out on the sidewalk. He was bleeding heavily from a deep laceration above his eye and he was arguing with a police officer. The man appeared to be highly intoxicated. He reportedly had made a racial comment to the store clerk, who then punched him in the eye and reportedly knocked him out for several minutes.

The medic introduced herself, empathically stated that she appreciated that he was having a tough time, and gently explained to the man that he

> *needed to go to the hospital because he had lost consciousness. She further indicated that she was concerned about his eye and wanted a doctor to take a look. While stumbling around, the man yelled back at the medic and said that he wasn't going anywhere. Police officers at the scene explained to the man that he could walk to the ambulance as a "gentleman," or else they would have to cuff him and drag him. He eventually walked on his own.*

In this case, efforts to "connect" with this man were fruitless due to apparent intoxication and his level of agitation. Noteworthy however, was that although the police department paramedic's efforts to engage the man appeared to be ineffective, many bystanders, including numerous teenagers, were impressed with her apparent sensitivity and calmness in dealing with him. One may go a step further in generalizing this point. Directly witnessing such a scene was traumatic for the bystanders. Observing the paramedic's apparent warmth and empathy might have been a healthy shot-in-the-arm for police/community relations.

The **alcohol/substance involved individual** presents a challenge to caregivers. Efforts to implement CATSM will likely be confounded by the influence of the substance itself. It is generally not advisable to make physical contact. Speak in a warm calming tone, avoid loud noises and bright lights (including flashlights), and assume a non-confrontative approach. Although CATSM should generally be implemented by one caregiver (as indicated previously), it may be advisable to approach the substance-involved person with assistance.

Intervention with an individual who is experiencing a "bad trip" should incorporate a calming tone and pleasant, relaxing imagery. Create a "scene" where there are friendly people, in a beautiful place, with pleasing sounds, sweet smells, etc. Attribute the reaction the person is experiencing to the substance, rather than to the individual himself. Assure him that he is not going crazy and that the effect of the drug will pass. Your intervention may ultimately stimulate a recognition that help in overcoming a substance abuse problem may come from others.

Intervention with a **violent, or potentially violent individual,** presents as another challenging opportunity. First, it may help to know that perhaps the best way of predicting whether an individual may become violent, is whether he has a history of violent behavior. Unfortunately, you may not have the luxury of knowing this information while at the scene of a traumatic event. If possible, separate the potentially violent individual from others. If he is acting-out, he may find others' reactions to his obstreperous behavior reinforcing. Always have another caregiver nearby if you need assistance. Take your time, move slowly and strive to establish a connection. Listen carefully, respond empathically and utilize cooperative statements such as, "I'd like to help you. Let's work together at this." Speaking in a calm supportive tone with good eye contact is critical.

Finally, a good rule of thumb is to have the potentially violent individual sit down. It is more difficult for someone to punch, kick or in some way strike-out at another person if he is seated. And, if he chose to do so, rising from a seated position may give you, or someone else, time to intervene. For example, when police officers are called to a home for a domestic dispute, efforts to engage the parties in a constructive discussion should be made with all parties in a seated position.

Just as substance involvement and dealing with a potentially violent individual may interfere with efforts to implement ATSM, so too will other factors specific to the individual. For example, consider **language and cultural factors.** These barriers to communication will certainly come into play when attempting to engage someone in discussion. Similarly, a **medical condition, physical injury** or **severe pain** may additionally taint efforts to communicate effectively.

While working with a **mentally challenged individual**, you will have to adjust your approach to address his cognitive and emotional needs. For instance, a mentally retarded adult may function cognitively and emotionally like a child. Consequently, his ability to comprehend the nature of what has occurred may be very limited and his coping strategies, very weak.

Helping **mentally disturbed individuals** will necessitate adjustments as well. Certainly, there are different levels of psychopathology and ATSM strategies can be implemented with most mentally disturbed people. Notwithstanding, paranoid, delusional, hallucinating individuals should be approached with caution. These individuals, who are evidencing signs of psychotic process, may become violent-particularly in the face of a traumatic event that overwhelms their limited, and oftentimes ineffective, coping abilities. At times, it may be difficult to discern the mentally disturbed person from the substance involved individual. There may also be comorbidity (i.e., the emotionally disturbed person who is under the influence of a substance).

In the wake of a **sexual assault,** as always, make sure that the individual's immediate safety is ensured and that physical injuries are being addressed. The sexual assault victim may have great difficulty communicating. Speak in a warm calm tone, focus on the here-and-now, assure the victim of safety, and avoid physical contact. Trust and control will likely be critical variables. Attempt to "give back" a sense of control by asking the victim if it is okay to proceed with a given action. For example, a paramedic might say, "I see that you're very uncomfortable. May I take a look at the cut?" Finally, recognize that a female victim may have particular difficulty speaking with a man. Having a female implement the ATSM process may help.

In working with young **children** who have been exposed to a traumatic event, you may need to hold and cuddle the child. Reassure him that he is safe. Know that young children will take cues from adults around them, particularly those with whom they are close, in responding to traumatic experiences. It is therefore important to separate children, as quickly as possible, from all stressors—including emotionally overwhelmed adults.

Engaging children must be made consistent with their developmental level. For example, offering more information than a child is cognitively able to manage may do more harm than good. Recognize that children, particularly young children, are generally unable to express their feelings verbally. They may likely convey their feelings through their behaviors/actions. If you have the time, providing children the opportunity to draw with crayons may be helpful. For example, you may encourage them to draw something that they remember about the event. The drawing may then be used as a vehicle to understand the thoughts and feeling the child is experiencing.

Children who are exposed to traumatic events may be likened to soft wet clay. Initially, the clay may be shaped and molded—but with time it begins to harden. When it does, one may take out a mallet and chisel and work to shape the clay. How much easier would it have been to have worked with that clay early on?

Working with **depressed, self-destructive and potentially suicidal** individuals will present a challenge for the emergency responder. First, recognize that people who talk about suicide are the ones who ultimately commit suicide. Take all threats seriously. If you believe that an individual is "only looking for attention," recognize that threatening to harm oneself is a very unhealthy way of seeking attention.

It may be necessary to transport a potentially self-destructive individual to a medical facility for psychiatric evaluation. It is not your job to assess if he is truly at-risk of harming himself. Rather, you should focus on initiating a process that will ultimately increase an individual's level of receptivity toward evaluation and intervention.

It is therefore important to separate children, as quickly as possible, from all stressors—including emotionally over-whelmed adults.

The following indicators may suggest a greater likelihood of self-destructive potential. Having a familiarity with these may help you to identify individuals who pose a greater risk for committing suicide:

- has previously attempted suicide
- has a history of self-destructive behavior
- is talking or writing about suicide
- has a specific plan
- has access to a gun or other lethal means
- is suffering from depression or other mental illness
- evidences a sudden change in personality/behavior
- has experienced a prior tragedy (e.g., suicide of family member)
- is involved with alcohol and/or other substance
- describes his situation as "hopeless"
- has sleep and/or eating disturbances
- is talking about "not being around…", saying good-bye
- gives away possessions, etc.

During a traumatic event it is unlikely that you will be aware of many critical individual characteristics. However, these characteristics may be revealed during interviews and investigations. Some of these individual characteristics suggest a greater likelihood for acute traumatic stress reactions and chronic stress disorders. The following is a list of "high-risk" indicators. It is recommended that you become familiar with these:

- prior exposure to severe adverse life events (e.g., combat)
- prior victimization (e.g., childhood sexual and physical abuse)
- significant losses
- close proximity to the event
- severity of the event itself
- extended exposure to danger
- pre-trauma anxiety and depression
- chronic medical condition

- substance involvement
- history of trouble with authority (e.g., stealing, vandalism, etc.)
- mental illness
- lack of familial/social support
- having no opportunity to vent (i.e., unable to tell one's story)
- strong emotional reactions upon exposure to the event
- perceived threat of danger to self/others
- physically injured by event

The unique characteristics of those you are called to serve will influence your ability to address their emergent psychological needs.

4. Characteristics of the Traumatic Event

The type of traumatic event will impact upon, or influence, your ability to address acute traumatic stress reactions. For example, during many events, all efforts must first be made to ensure the safety and well-being of everyone involved. The following are examples of events that may call for these safety and/or life-saving measures:

- fires or chemical spills
- suicide attempts
- substance overdoses
- acute medical conditions
- child or elder abuse or neglect
- sexual assaults and sexual molestation
- violence (e.g., gang fight, domestic violence, assaults, etc.)
- sniper attacks, terrorist attacks and hostage situations
- nuclear, biological or chemical (NBC) threats/activity
- plane, train, boat, bus or automobile accidents, and
- natural disasters (e.g., tornado, flood, earthquake, etc.).

Generally, as the severity of a traumatic event increases, so does the level of traumatic stress.

Generally, as the severity of a traumatic event increases, so does the level of traumatic stress. For example, people who experience severe traumatic exposure (e.g., rape) often manifest traumatic stress symptomatology and frequently go on to develop traumatic stress disorders. However, as described previously, there are many factors that will influence how an individual will ultimately respond to traumatic events.

How Can We Helping Grieving Individuals?

Grief refers to the feelings that are precipitated by loss. The early reactions that we see in grieving individuals occur during a period of "Numbing." Initially, the individual may present in shock. There may be a highly anxious, active response with an outburst of extremely intense distress or perhaps a seemingly stunned, emotionally-numb response.

During this early phase, you may likely observe denial—an inability to acknowledge the impact of the event or perhaps, that the event has occurred. The individual may evidence dissociation, in which he may seem dazed and apathetic, and he may express feelings of unreality. It is not unusual for people to make statements such as, "I can't believe it," "This is not happening," "This has got to be a bad dream," etc. Finally, there may be periods of intense emotion (e.g., crying, screaming, rage, anger, fear, guilt, etc.). Recognize that these kinds of reactions to a traumatic loss are normal responses.

Within hours or perhaps days of the loss, "Yearning and Searching" may be observed. Here, the individual begins to register the reality of the loss. There may be a preoccupation with the lost individual. Symptoms may include, but not be limited to, insomnia, poor appetite, headaches, anxiety, tension, anger, guilt, etc. Sounds and signals may be interpreted as the deceased person's presence.

Within weeks to months following the loss is a period of "Disorganization." Here, feelings of anger and depression are exhibited. The individual may likely pose questions (e.g., "Why did this have to happen?") and evidence periods of "bargaining" (e.g., "If only I could see him just one last time."). Finally, in the months or even years following the loss is a time of "Reorganization." Here, the individual begins to accept the loss-often cultivating new life patterns and goals.

There are no "cookbook" approaches to helping people who are struggling with loss. Perhaps the most important variable is "being there" for the person. Attempt to connect with the him using the ATSM model. Encourage expression of thoughts and feelings without insistence. Recognize that although relatives and friends intend to be supportive, they may be inclined to discourage the expression of feelings-particularly anger and guilt. Avoidance of such expression may prolong the grieving process and can be counterproductive. Allow periods of silence and be careful not to lecture.

When working with grieving individuals, avoid cliches such as "Be strong," and "You're doing so well." Such cliches may only serve to reinforce an individual's feelings of aloneness. Again, allow the bereaved to tell you how they feel and attempt to "normalize" grief reactions. Finally, don't be afraid to touch. A squeeze of the hand, a gentle pat on the back or a warm embrace can show you are there and that you truly care.

Practical Guidelines for Assisting the Grieving Individual

- Provide opportunities for ventilation of emotions.

- Provide support and availability at funeral.

- Practice active and empathic listening (e.g., show acceptance of the feelings and experiences of the griever)

- Provide the individual with an opportunity to reminisce and reflect on their deceased significant other.

- Keep tissues visible and available.

- Encourage the individual to maintain proper care and nurturance for themselves.

- Educate the individual regarding the reactions that they may experience over the next few weeks and/or months (e.g., sleep difficulty, anger, etc.).

- Assist with out-of-work interventions/referrals if indicated. Consider referral to an Employee Assistance Program (EAP).

- Refer for medical consultation in the event of severe insomnia or physical reactions (e.g., migraine headaches).

- Remain mindful for signs that the individual is not coping well (e.g., suicidal threats) and seek medical and/or familial involvement.

- Be mindful of your own feelings surrounding death and know your limitations in your effort to assist the individual.

CHAPTER FIVE

Comprehensive Acute Traumatic Stress Management

The Application of Acute Traumatic Stress Management Within Organizations

Organizational crises take many forms, each having the potential to disrupt individuals' and the organization's ability to function. A crisis in the life of a staff member may be personal, such as the loss of a loved one, an accident or diagnosis of serious illness. A crisis may also result from an event outside of the workplace that affects many workers, such a hurricane, a terrorist bombing, or an accident. Lastly, a crisis may be the result of direct or indirect exposure to a powerful incident during the performance of work. Regardless of the cause, the organization will be disrupted. Immediate action must be taken to care for staff in order to maintain the organization's ability to function. Consider the following incident:

At 2:30am a power plant worker entered a switching room to carry out a routine procedure. In the process, something went wrong—an explosion occurred. The sound of the blast was heard throughout the plant causing immediate concern in all workers. As a result of the explosion, the worker suffered third degree burns over 80% of his body.

Despite his critical burns, the worker remained conscious, exited the switching room and began to walk through the power plant to the first aid area. His clothing had been burned off, his skin was blackened, blistered and raw. As he moved toward the first aid area he passed workers who looked on in horror. One of the workers commented that he looked like "the walking dead" in a horror film. Every man who encountered him was shocked by the sight and smell of burned flesh. None of these men were prepared for what they saw and all felt helpless, not knowing how to assist him.

Halfway to the first aid area he collapsed. Those who were walking with him did not know what to do—they feared touching him. The first aid team arrived and reported feeling completely overwhelmed. They were well schooled in basic first aid and CPR techniques; they were not prepared to treat the magnitude of this worker's injuries. They did what they could for him and awaited the arrival of EMS.

He was transported to the medical center, where he died from his burns 18 hours later.

Organizational Impact

All workers need to be provided with information and assistance in managing the traumatic stress the incident created.

An event such as the one described above will negatively impact the organization's ability to function. During the incident, and in the days and weeks following an event of this magnitude, it will not be "business as usual."

While the mission of the organization must continue, the normal routine will be disrupted. Those most severely affected need to be identified quickly. All workers need to be provided with information and assistance in managing the traumatic stress the incident created. There should be a family liaison at the hospital and funeral home, and daily updates provided to all workers to control rumors—thus lessening "fear of the unknown." Through all of this, the organization must continue to function safely and efficiently, carrying out its daily routines.

In the aftermath of a traumatic event, it is common for delayed stress reactions to occur, creating a level of dysfunction. Workers are at-risk for stress reactions that may compromise safety and the ability to think clearly, focus and concentrate. Managers and supervisors are trained to "get the job done." However, the workers must do the job. The challenge facing management during a traumatic incident is, first and foremost, to manage stress and safety issues thus enabling the organization to continue to function safely and productively. Management needs to recognize that the effect of such powerful events can linger, causing performance, behavior and safety issues in the weeks and months following the incident.

When organizational/workplace crises occur, it is of the utmost importance that the organization responds to the needs of the staff. The working environment produces many significant personal relationships, with strong bonds and lasting friendships. For many individuals, the workplace becomes a "family" environment, a place where many hours are spent, often for a worker's entire career spanning 20 to 30 or more years. Despite the complex nature of one's work, and the difficulty that may be encountered on a daily basis, the workplace becomes a comfortable, predictable, safe place. An event such as the one described above shakes the basic foundation of safety and predictability, creating a sense of fear and threat to security.

Workplace trauma results from events that cause significant distress among staff. Examples of traumatic events include, but are not limited to, the following:

- Serious injury or death of a coworker
- Staff member injured as a result of another staff member's actions
- Violence/assault by coworker
- Large number of staff injured in a workplace accident
- Sudden death on an employee while off duty
- Suicide of a coworker
- Harassment of an employee
- Employee diagnosed with a serious illness requiring hospitalization

- Down-sizing and organizational restructuring that drastically impacts staff
- National events such as terror incidents with media coverage
- Mass causality incidents
- Serious injury or death to children
- In the hospital setting, prolonged involvement/attachment with a patient's family.

After learning of a crisis situation, it is imperative that the organization responds immediately. The *Connect, Ground, Support, Normalize* and *Prepare* stages of ATSM, outlined in the previous chapter, may be applied at an organizational level as *Comprehensive* Acute Traumatic Stress Management.

Traumatic events can create a variety of reactions in staff members. These reactions may include a sense of vulnerability, fear, anxiety, anger, betrayal, confusion, threat, guilt and abandonment. Additionally, traumatic events that impact organizations may result in:

- Fear of danger and concern for personal injury, not present prior to the incident
- A desire to isolate from coworkers
- A breakdown in communication
- A decrease in morale and group cohesiveness
- Anger and resentment toward management
- Irritability and development of a "poor attitude" toward the organization and coworkers
- Employee sabotage
- Increased illness and use of sick leave
- An increase in health care costs
- Workers' compensation and disability claims
- Employee litigation
- Increased error level
- An inability to retain effective personnel
- Safety issues caused by loss of focus and ability to concentrate
- Increase in resignations and retirement
- A marked decrease in productivity.

After learning of a crisis situation, it is imperative that the organization responds immediately. The *Connect, Ground, Support, Normalize* and *Prepare*

stages of ATSM, outlined in the previous chapter, may be applied at an organizational level as *Comprehensive* Acute Traumatic Stress Management (CATSM). Following, is a discussion of the Three Phases of CATSM.

The Three Phases of CATSM

Workplace trauma has the potential to strike at any time. Notwithstanding, traumatic incidents, while frightening and disruptive, can be effectively managed. Comprehensive Acute Traumatic Stress Management (CATSM) provides a framework to effectively address crises in organizations *before, during* and *after* a traumatic event. CATSM is a three-phase approach which includes: **1) Planning** (i.e., prior to the incident) **2) Engagement** (i.e., during the event) and **3) Disengagement** (i.e., after the event). These phases enable CATSM to *prepare, stabilize* and *recover* individuals and organizations due to exposure to a traumatic event.

Planning

This initial phase reflects the expansion of the ATSM model described in Chapter Three. It aims to empower organizations by providing practical information, education and training *before* a traumatic event occurs. The Planning phase of CATSM includes the development and implementation of the following:

- **Stress Awareness Program for Management:** This program provides general stress management information. It prepares administrators, managers and supervisors to recognize the effect stress has on safety and performance, and provides basic intervention strategies. Additionally, this program provides practical information concerning the effects of *traumatic* stress and offers specific strategies for managing a traumatic incident. The primary goal is to maintain staff safety and the ability to function.

In Comprehensive Acute Traumatic Stress Management (CATSM), we expand the scope of ATSM to enable us to assist *organizations* during a crisis.

- **Stress Management Training for Staff:** This program is designed to assist staff members in managing the stress of life at home and in the workplace. This training additionally includes basic information regarding the emotional, cognitive, behavioral, physiological and spiritual experiences of individuals who are exposed to traumatic events.

- **Organizational Traumatic Incident Management Team (OTIM):** Prior to a traumatic incident, an OTIM can be developed. This team can respond to the immediate needs of distressed staff during and in the aftermath of a traumatic event. The OTIM utilizes the CATSM model to meet the emergent needs of individuals and the organization during times of crisis.

- **Family Support Program:** This program, developed prior to a traumatic event, is designed to assist workers' families during and in the aftermath of a crisis. Workplace incidents impact workers' families—and the family environment impacts the workplace.

Engagement and Disengagement

As described previously, the traumatic stress-specific components of the Acute Traumatic Stress Management (ATSM) model are implemented through stages where we *Observe and Identify*, and then *Connect* with, *Ground*, *Support*, *Normalize* and *Prepare* individuals who have been exposed to a traumatic incident. These basic stages of ATSM may be provided by management, supervisors, medical and health care staff, support staff or any other caregiver trained in the process. ATSM addresses emergent psychological needs, keeps people functioning and, ultimately, strives to mitigate long-term emotional suffering. In Comprehensive Acute Traumatic Stress Management (CATSM), we expand the scope of ATSM to enable us to assist *organizations* during a crisis. Each of the stages offers specific guidelines enabling an organization to work-through a traumatic incident.

It is important to note that some organizations call-in outside teams of "experts" during times of crisis. CATSM, provided by an Organizational Traumatic Incident Management Team (OTIM), draws upon the collaborative relationships that exist among members of an organizational family. It enables the organization to respond immediately and empowers the organization to address to the needs of their staff. Crises present tremendous opportunities for growth—even if that opportunity is not immediately realized or understood. The manner in which organizational management responds to a crisis will be remembered forever.

There may be times when an organization's ability to respond is taxed and overwhelmed (e.g., a mass casualty incident impacting the workplace, an incident that directly affects management and OTIM members, etc.). During these events, the efficacy of calling-in outside crisis management teams should be weighed.

As soon as anyone within the organization becomes aware of a crisis situation, management must be informed. The initial response from the organization should focus on stabilization. An assessment of the impact of the incident on the organization will be ongoing as the hours go by. During this time, every effort should be made to keep people functioning safely and productively.

The manner in which organizational management responds to a crisis will be remembered forever.

It is critical to underscore the importance of addressing potentially life-threatening physical needs *prior* to emotional needs. Following is an overview of the application of CATSM:

1) Connect

During this initial stage, the organization must reach out to all staff to identify their location and assess their immediate safety. Managers and supervisors who have been trained in the CATSM process should work to connect with their staff and assess their physical and psychological needs.

Through the ATSM process, described in Chapter Three, managers and supervisors can begin immediate intervention, providing stabilization for staff, insuring safety and helping to preserve the organization's ability to function.

The first questions to be asked by management, supervisors and members of the OTIM should be, **"Are you okay?" "What can I do for you?"** and **"How can I help you?"** Connecting with staff with these questions demonstrates a genuine concern for the person, not the job.

During this early stage, a connection should be established with families. When necessary (e.g., incidents involving serious injury with hospitalization or death), a liaison should be established to assist the family. This liaison can provide information, assist with transportation etc. A connection with families may also be established through a letter that provides information regarding facts concerning the incident, stress management information, guidelines for speaking with children regarding the incident and a resource of referrals that may be used to assist the family in managing the traumatic event. Key organization phone numbers (i.e. OTIM team leader, administrative representative, human resources, employee assistance etc.) should be provided.

During long-term incident engagement (e.g., disasters, storms, terrorist incidents) it is imperative that staff remain connected with their families. If it is appropriate and practical, staff may contact their family to be reassured they are okay. It is important to realize that staff members will not be able to provide productive service if there is constant worry and concern for the safety and well being of their family.

Always remember that connecting is an ongoing process during a traumatic incident.

2) Ground

Grounding, at the organizational level, works to keep staff informed with facts. During this stage, staff is provided with information concerning what is known about the incident and what needs to be done at an organizational level. Through the provision of facts, staff members are prevented from cultivating destructive and irrational beliefs and assumptions that can lead to emotional distress. Grounding will help to prevent rumors, and will give staff a sense of safety and security by lessening the "fear of the unknown."

Grounding will help to prevent rumors, and will give staff a sense of safety and security by lessening the "fear of the unknown."

During this time, scheduled updates should be provided. Staff members need to know that they will be kept informed. Updates can take the form of staff meetings, e-mail, postings, a letter, etc. Updates are extremely important when a staff member has been injured or has become critically ill. Information regarding the worker's medical status should protect the privacy of the individual and take into consideration the wishes of the worker's family. This information is important to alleviate fears and concerns of coworkers.

Finally, recognize that the provision of factual information gives back a sense of control that a crisis seems to have taken away. This is exemplified in a staff member's statement, "At least I knew what I was dealing with."

3) Support

Ongoing support may be formal or informal. Concern and support for the staff should be demonstrated early in the incident. During this phase, management has the opportunity to let staff know that they care about the safety and well-being of the organizational family. It is interesting to note that worker motivation stems primarily from recognition of individuals who are appreciated for who they are and what they do. During a time of crisis, a golden opportunity exists for management to show that they care and are concerned about the people who work for them. Always remember, the action taken by management during a traumatic incident will be etched in the minds of staff forever.

Simple statements and questions, introduced in the previous connecting stage of CATSM, should continue (e.g., "How are you?", "What can I do for you?" "Are you okay?"). Empathic statements, such as, "I see this is a difficult time—I'll do whatever I can to help," will go a long way in providing support for staff.

Support is perhaps best demonstrated by a continued presence that allows for the connection between staff and management. Depending upon the magnitude of the incident, the degree of danger involved and the disruption created, staff may feel isolated and fearful. Having leaders present provides control and direction which, in and of itself, is a powerful demonstration of support. It conveys that during this time of great distress, "we are in this together." Support may be provided individually or in a group setting. It may take the form of informal conversation, centering around facts, or it may be more formal, scheduled *Informational Supportive Briefings (ISB)*. The ISB is a process that integrates the final three stages of CATSM for an organization. It will be discussed, in detail, shortly.

Finally, support also needs to be extended to the families of staff. When required, mental health support services should be made available as well as ISB sessions. This may be accomplished through Employee Assistance Programs, or may be provided by OTIM team members.

4) Normalize

Staff will experience various symptoms and reactions to the traumatic incident. These reactions may not be understood and may be perceived as abnormal. It is through a process of education that we are able to normalize and validate the reactions and symptoms that are being experienced. Our primary goal during this normalization stage is to help people to know that *their* responses are normal given the presence of an abnormal event. The normalization process helps to keep people functioning and may ultimately help to mitigate long-term traumatic stress reactions. Normalization and validation may be facilitated in organizations through the provision of *Informational Supportive Briefings* (ISB)—to be discussed shortly.

5) Prepare

During the Engagement phase of CATSM, events occur and change rapidly, representing a period of uncertainty. As described previously, this uncertainty creates a "fear of the unknown"—often leaving staff feeling vulnerable and insecure. Preparation for upcoming events and activities is paramount to lessening these concerns and fears, and provides a degree of structure. Staff will be prepared if routine ISBs are provided, schedules are established, daily plans are outlined and short range goals are presented. Direction empowers the staff to move forward as uncertainty disappears.

The Disengagement Briefing is an individual or small group meeting conducted immediately prior to staff being released from work following a traumatic incident.

Disengagement Briefings may be utilized by the organization in order to prepare staff for what may lie on the road ahead. The Disengagement Briefing is an individual or small group meeting conducted immediately prior to staff being released from work following a traumatic incident. It is an assessment of staff needs—physical condition, ability to safely travel home and the opportunity to provide organization and stress management information. Brief discussion of the incident is encouraged and questions are answered. A supervisor and OTIM member should conduct Disengagement Briefings.

Informational Supportive Briefing (ISB)

As introduced previously, the ISB is a process that integrates the final three stages of CATSM (i.e. *Support, Normalize* and *Prepare*) for an organization within a group format. The ISB is conducted by administrative staff and the OTIM and may be repeated multiple times throughout the Engagement and Disengagement phases. It serves to maintain a connection between management and staff, is a vehicle for providing information, support, normalization of stress reactions and preparation for the future. The ISB may be conducted with both large and small groups and takes the form of an educational session, which encourages brief group discussion. This process helps staff to begin to cultivate an understanding of how and why the incident occurred. It assists in organizing the events into a "story" format and provides stress management information. Administrative staff provides factual organizational information in order to keep staff updated.

ISB sessions are scheduled and all staff should be required to attend. ISBs should be repeated as often as necessary. The session is opened by senior management in the spirit of concern for the well-being of staff and a brief overview of the intent of the session is provided. OTIM members are introduced and given the opportunity to comment briefly about the importance of addressing the stress created by the incident.

Following this brief introductory period, administrative personnel present factual information regarding the incident. This information will include what is known about the event, update on injured staff, organization activity such as staff schedules, daily plans etc. OTIM members are then introduced and given the opportunity to present information regarding traumatic stress. Signs and symptoms suggestive of traumatic stress reactions are presented in conjunction with appropriate stress management techniques. Stress management handout materials are provided to staff to bring home to their families in order to assist them in managing the event (see Appendix C).

Staff members are given the opportunity to ask questions, discuss stress reactions and raise concerns. Finally, information regarding immediate future organizational plans and support programs are announced. Contact phone numbers for OTIM members and key management personnel are provided. These phone contacts are crucial in order to maintain the staff's sense of connection to the organization. The session is then formally closed. It is important that administrative staff and OTIM members make themselves available for individual conversation, thus maintaining connection, availability and support.

Family Support

Workplace incidents negatively impact home life. Caring for the family of a staff member who is injured or dies while on the job demonstrates a concern for the worth and value of the individual. Additionally, when staff sees that they are appreciated, and are cared about by the organization, motivation and productivity often increase. The following basic services should be considered:

- Provide Organizational Traumatic Incident Management Team (OTIM) support at the home, hospital or funeral home.
- Designate administrative staff member to serve as liaison in order to keep the lines of communication open. Visit the family frequently during the period of incident engagement to answer questions.
- Provide transportation to and from the hospital / funeral home if required. Offer to provide airport pickup for relatives arriving from out of state.
- Provide resources and strategies for stress management.
- Provide childcare.
- Provide family intervention/referral through Human Resources and Employee Assistance Programs.

Summary

Comprehensive Acute Traumatic Stress Management provides a framework to effectively address crises before, during and after a traumatic event. Through a three phase approach including Planning, Engagement, and Disengagement CATSM *Prepares, Stabilizes* and *Recovers* individuals, groups and organizations. The CATSM process empowers people to regain control during a period of marked disruption and enables the organization to survive and thrive.

CHAPTER SIX

Practical Application for Serious Injury/Death Notification for Emergency Responders, Healthcare Professionals, Educators, the Clergy and Organizational Management

For many of us, when we think of serious injury and death notification, images of police officers knocking on the front door to someone's home comes to mind. Alternatively, we may envision a notification being made in a hospital setting. However, serious injury and death notification may be required in the workplace following accidents or sudden death situations. Consider the following incident:

> *A 20-year employee of a bank branch was killed in an auto accident on Saturday night. This individual was held in high regard by all members of the staff, and in fact had served as the bank's training officer for many years. She was considered by most to be a true friend. Police personnel were required to respond to her home in order to make the death notification to family. Additionally, the branch manager was notified by her family of the death on Sunday evening—necessitating a "death notification" to the staff on Monday morning.*

Serious injury and death notification are among the most difficult challenges we face. The anxiety produced by these notifications comes from a lack of training and experience in this area, personnel identifying with the survivors' distress, and a fear of survivors' emotional and physical reactions to the notification.

While these notifications are extremely difficult for individuals who must present this information, it must be remembered that for the survivors this is the first and only time they will receive this news regarding the injured or deceased. For them, it is their worst fear come true. How the notification is actually made, and the nature of support that is subsequently provided, will directly influence the survivors' adjustment and recovery. Remember that communication is the key to a successful notification. The words spoken with survivors during the notification will have lasting impact. Always keep in mind that you are not hurting people. Rather, the *message* that you are conveying is hurtful. Finally, consider how you would like your family treated should a notification be made to them.

How the notification is actually made, and the nature of support that is subsequently provided, will directly influence the survivors' adjustment and recovery.

The following information is provided for emergency responders, healthcare professionals, educators, the clergy and organizational management. It offers a method for the safe and effective delivery of the Serious Injury/Death Notification. Realize that no two notifications will be the same. Adjustments must be made to address the unique characteristics of the individuals involved (e.g., language barriers, cultural factors, physical condition of the survivors, etc.), as well as the nature of the situation itself (e.g., natural disaster, homicide, automobile accident, etc.).

It is particularly important that you consider *your* ability to make the notification. If you have recently experienced a significant loss, have experienced the personal notification of a serious injury or death, or are currently experiencing a significant life stress issue, you may not be emotionally prepared to face the raw expression of survivor emotion that may be present. Make your immediate supervisor aware of your concern.

1. **Assignment of Staff**

    A. **Emergency Service notifications:**

    In determining who should make the notification, consider the following:

    1. Select two staff members who are familiar with this notification process and with the ATSM model.

2. If possible, assign a male and a female.

3. Have at least one of the notifiers trained as a CFR or EMT in the event of a medical emergency.

4. Having a uniformed police officer present (i.e., when realistically possible) may decrease the potential for a violent reaction by the survivor(s).

5. Both notifiers should have knowledge of all available facts surrounding the event.

6. Staff selected should be prepared to spend as much time as required to provide support. Do not assign staff whose shift will end shortly.

B. **Workplace notifications**

1. Administration, highly respected management, or trained members of the Organization Traumatic Incident Management Team (OTIM) should be selected to make notification to staff.

2. OTIM members and employee assistance personnel should be present to manage emotional distress that may be present in staff members following notification.

2. **The Three Components of the Serious Injury/ Death Notification Process**
   A. Preparation
   B. Presentation
   C. Provision of ATSM

A. **Preparation**

Obtain all available facts. Serious Injury/Death notification requires accuracy regarding the nature of the incident, time and place of occurrence, who the victim is and where the victim currently is located. It is imperative that you have full details regarding the identity of the victim. For example, notifying a family that, "Your daughter has been killed in an accident," without knowing the full name of the victim, can create immediate confusion if there is more than one daughter currently not home. Realize that survivors may have a strong need to gather details in order to attempt to make sense of what has occurred. Answer questions honestly. If you do not know the answer to a question, acknowledge that you do not know. If possible, assist the survivor(s) in finding the answer.

Attempt to determine if there is any significant medical condition present in the survivor(s). For example, a cardiac condition may prove devastating in the presence of this powerful, negative news. Always have a radio and/or cellular phone with you. Be prepared to provide emergency care following the Serious Injury/Death notification. Consider having an ambulance standby near the location where the notification will be made. In a medical facility, alert the charge nurse, or other member of the medical team, that you will be engaging in a notification. Be sure to provide your exact location.

Never inform children of a Serious Injury or Death. Children should never be placed in the position of being the first to receive the news, and they should never be asked to carry this information to adults when they arrive home. Whenever possible, notify parents prior to notifying older siblings. Also, never use a child to interpret a language barrier. In this situation, you are asking the child to process the news and then explain to the adult. Locate an adult to translate the information. Never notify neighbors. Attempt to locate the survivor(s) in order to conduct the notification. Neighbors should never be notified before survivors.

Finally, never make a notification alone. In route, or in a medical facility, discuss your thoughts and feelings regarding this assignment with your notification partner. Preplan your method of delivery considering which of you is better able to present the notification. Review the facts carefully.

Workplace notifications require management to gather as many facts about the incident as possible. Provide staff with accurate information regarding the incident (i.e. when the accident or death occurred, nature of injuries, hospital visiting, wake and funeral details, and any special requests family has made). When providing information about injuries or medical status, be careful not to violate a person's privacy. Additionally, consider the possible emotional impact the notification may have on staff members who had a close relationship with the injured or deceased. Be prepared to provide support to these individuals. Notifications should be performed following the guidelines presented in the next section.

B. Presentation

1. Emergency Service Notifications

- Introduce yourself and your partner, and state your titles and/or positions.

- Gain access to the home. Do not make a notification on the doorstep. If you are in another setting such as a medical facility, find a private location.

- Attempt to determine who the family spokesperson is (e.g., spouse, father, elder sibling, etc.).

- Determine whom you are talking to. Ask, "Are you Mr...., Mrs..., the parents of..., the wife of..., the husband of..., the daughter of...?"

- Do not make the notification in the presence of young children. Request that they leave the room if possible.

- If a close friend or relative is available, consider having them join a sole survivor so he/she will not be alone.

- Have the survivor(s) sit down. Sit down with them and move close to them. Establish eye contact, lower your voice and use a warm gentle tone.

- Gently prepare the survivor for what is to come. Provide information honestly and directly. **1) Begin with a general statement.** For example, you might say, "Your husband Richard has been involved in a serious accident." Pause, allow this information to register. **Then, 2) follow with a more detailed, yet straight forward statement.** For example, "His car was struck by a large truck." Pause, allow this information to register. **Then, 3) provide the notification that the victim has died.** For example, "Richard died as a result of his injuries." Pause, allow this information to register. If necessary repeat the information. You may next state, "I'm sorry... I will stay with you, I won't leave you alone."

- When making a death notification it is very important to be direct using the word, "died." This word has universal meaning. Do not use terms like, "He passed away," "He has left us," or "He has expired." Do not leave any room for misinterpretation. Always use the victim's name and never refer to the victim with words like "body," "corpse" or "the deceased." These are impersonal and cold, and may convey a lack of sensitivity on your part.

- When the notification involves what appears to be a suicide, do not label the cause of death a "suicide" unless an official determination has been made. Instead, describe the nature of the event. For example, you might say, "Mary was found in her bathtub with her wrists cut." If the survivor(s) asks you whether it was "a suicide," and an official determination has not been made, inform them that the cause of death is being investigated. Be careful not to blame or judge what appears to be a suicide.

2. **Workplace Notifications**

- Have staff report to a central location such as conference room, cafeteria, etc.

- Attempt to relax the environment as much as possible. Eliminate a formal presentation appearance.

- Utilize the previous information for Emergency Service notifications. In case example cited previously, the presentation may take the following format:

"On Saturday evening Mary Walters was involved in a serious car accident. She was apparently heading home on Route 44 from a dinner engagement when her car skidded off the road and hit a tree. She sustained serious head trauma as result of the impact and was transported to the medical center. As a result of her injuries, Mary died in the emergency room at 4:30am Saturday morning."

Present this information slowly and with compassion. Avoid the appearance of indifference or an uncaring attitude. Provide information regarding wake services and funeral. Discuss any requests the deceased family has made such as donations, flowers, etc.

- Allow time for staff to process the information and be prepared to answer questions.

- Be alert to staff members who may be extremely distressed and offer support as required.

- When possible, consider allowing staff time to attend the funeral service.

C. **The Provision of ATSM**

Once the notification is made, utilize the ATSM model. The latter three stages, "Support," "Normalize the Response" and "Prepare for the Future," will be highly applicable here.

As indicated early in this publication, specific emotional, cognitive, behavioral, physiological and spiritual reactions may be exhibited by people during traumatic exposure (see Chapter One). These are normal responses to an abnormal event. Following a Serious Injury/Death Notification, be prepared for a cascade of the most intense levels of emotion. Allow tears, anger and frustration. However, do not allow the survivors to harm themselves or others—including yourself. If you find yourself becoming teary-eyed, realize that it is okay for you to display emotion. Your reaction demonstrates your humanness and compassion for the survivor(s). Be alert for physical distress and provide emergency care as required. If the survivor takes medication, assist them with this process.

- Ask whether there is someone you can call to come to the location. If possible, arrange for transportation for this person. Following a workplace notification where staff members are extremely distressed, assess their ability to leave the workplace safely. Obtain assistance for distressed staff if required.

- Be prepared to spend as much time as is required. Do not rush this process or give the impression you have something else to do.

- Encourage family members and staff to be together and offer resources for help (e.g., clergy and/or counseling), if needed.

- Regarding a family notification, do not allow the survivor to drive if they are required to leave the location.

- Never leave the survivor alone.

Special Considerations for Emergency Service Notifications

- **Notification at place of business.** If it necessary to make the Serious Injury/Death notification at a place of business, locate management personnel, identify yourself, and inform them that you must speak with [name] in private. Reveal minimal information regarding the incident only if it is necessary to gain access to the survivor. Following the notification, make arrangements to take the survivor home, to the hospital or other determined location. Under no circumstance allow the survivor to drive.

- **Telephone notification.** Make every effort to notify by personal contact, not by telephone. Telephone contact is impersonal and does not allow for adequate support. If, however, it is the only way possible to make the notification, do the following. Find someone to be with the survivor when the call comes. Consider calling local clergy, a physician, neighbor or family friend. Inform in straightforward simple language as described previously. Be honest and be patient. Following the notification, speak with the person called to be with the survivor and provide any information necessary.

- **Language barrier.** Prior to notification, attempt to determine if a language barrier exists and arrange to be accompanied by an interpreter. As previously discussed, do not use children to provide interpretation and if possible, do not use family members to provide interpretation.

- **Cultural concerns.** Death is a universal event for humans. Reactions to this event will vary based on culture. It is not always possible for the notifier to have knowledge of the varied cultural reactions that may be demonstrated. However, the basic steps discussed in this publication may be applied universally across cultures.

- **Additional victims at scene.** When confronted with surviving victims at the scene of traumatic events who are aware of other victims injuries, you must consider the appropriateness of their receiving negative news. Consider if they can tolerate the information without incurring serious physical or psychological distress. Determine if they are able to understand the information. And finally, determine if the information may worsen their medical condition. If you believe providing negative information will complicate the situation while at the scene, provide "safe details." For example, if you are asked, "Is my wife dead?" respond, "They are working on her right now-I will find out more information as soon as I can." If the survivor is aware that death has occurred and asks, "She is dead, isn't she?" be honest and state "Yes, she has died as a result of her injuries; I'm sorry." Follow the protocol as described previously. Assure the survivor that you will stay with him and continue with necessary medical care.

Do's and Don'ts of Serious Injury/Death Notification

Do use statements like...

"I'm sorry."

"I'm here for you and I won't leave you alone."

"You are responding like a *normal* person trying to deal with an *abnormal* experience."

"It's like you're trying to make sense of the senseless."

"This is so much harder than most people think."

"It's okay to feel."

Do not use statements that take control away.

"You don't need to see him."

"That is information you don't need to know."

"It is best to remember her the way she was."

"I'm not able to tell you that."

Do not use statements that patronize/discount.

"Someday you will get over this."

"It could have been much worse; your daughter is still alive."

"It was just the wrong place to be at that time."

"Accidents happen."

"Time heals all wounds."

"I know this is difficult, but you must go on with your life."

"I know how you feel. Now you must hold on to your memories."

"He never knew what hit him."

Do not use religious clichés.

"It must have been his time."

"God gives us only what we can handle."

"Prayer heals all wounds."

"He's in heaven now."

"It was a blessing given how bad his injuries were."

Following the Serious Injury/Death Notification

Following the notification, it is important that you debrief from the experience. Talk with your partner about the notification. Share your personal thoughts, reactions and feelings. Know that it is okay not to feel okay. If possible, talk with a counselor and allow yourself to release the experience in a healthy way.

Serious Injury/Death Notification is among the most difficult tasks for emergency responders—or anyone charged with this responsibility. There is no easy way to present a family, parent, spouse or staff with this devastating news. Your ability to communicate effectively and provide effective support with ATSM will directly influence the survivors' adjustment and recovery. A notification delivered in a safe, compassionate manner may very well be the first step toward healing for the survivors.

Always debrief following a notification and understand the potential for your own traumatic stress reaction.

They will never forget the pain of their loss—nor will they forget how they were informed. Consider your own needs in accepting the assignment and recovering from providing the notification. A recent loss in your life, a similar experience of being notified, or a current major life stress should preclude you from being part of this difficult process. Always debrief following a notification and understand the potential for your own traumatic stress reaction.

CHAPTER SEVEN

Helping *Ourselves* in the Aftermath of a Tragedy

Addressing the emergent psychological needs of others during a traumatic event can be a draining experience. Working with individuals who are in acute emotional distress requires an intensity that, for the caregiver, is both mental and physical. It is imperative that you consider your own state of mind prior to engaging in the provision of ATSM/CATSM. As indicated previously, if you are currently experiencing a time of emotional distress in your life, it would be wise to have another caregiver assist the victim(s). In this way, you lessen your chance of becoming victimized yourself by the event.

First responders will likely be exposed to the very events that they are called upon to help others. For example, after arriving at an automobile accident, a police officer had the responsibility of preserving the scene. While holding back bystanders, he provided psychological support. Yet he, too, had seen a gruesome, dismembered body on the roadway. First responders are often exposed to seemingly overwhelming physical events, as well as the psychological impact that these events have on others.

There will be times when you will identify personally or "link with" an individual with whom you are working—or perhaps with some aspect of the situation. For example, a young police detective was called upon to deliver a death notification to the parents of a 10 year-old girl. After sharing the news, she and her partner offered support for the grieving parents. Her feelings of discomfort shifted very quickly to feelings of being overwhelmed when she saw a photograph of the deceased child—the girl looked very much like her own daughter.

> **First responders are often exposed to seemingly overwhelming physical events, as well as the psychological impact that these events have on others.**

101

Despite drawing upon a specific strategy that will help you to remain "professionally detached," powerful thoughts and feelings have a way of piercing "professional detachment." This is a normal response to an abnormal situation.

If you find yourself feeling emotionally overwhelmed during the provision of ATSM, try the following:

During the Event

- Become aware of and monitor your emotional, cognitive, behavioral, physiological and spiritual reactions. Consider the effect the event is having on you. Acknowledge to yourself that your involvement is creating these reactions.

- If you find that the discussion is causing you to react physically (i.e., rapid heart rate, breathing increase, sweating, etc.) take a slow deep breath and tell yourself to relax—take a second deep breath and relax. If you are finding the event overwhelming, and it is possible, separate and share your feelings with a colleague.

- Realize that acute traumatic stress may compromise your ability to make good decisions and can therefore place you in danger. If you find that you are unable to concentrate, focus on the individual and the specific words they are saying—work to actively listen to what they are communicating. Slow down the conversation and try repeating what you have just heard.

- Acknowledge and speak of the impact the event is having on you as a human being. For example following the sudden death of a beloved colleague, you might say, "This is really tough for all of us...." However, make every effort to avoid self-disclosure of specific, personal information with others (e.g., "I remember during my first year here when another worker was killed in a car accident...."). Remember that it is okay not to be okay, and that displaying your emotions can reinforce for victims your genuine concern.

Following the Event

- Acknowledge that the event itself and the connections you have established with others can have a lasting impact on you. Words people have spoken and the emotions they displayed may become imprinted in your mind.

- Reflect upon what has just occurred. Maintain an awareness of your emotional, cognitive, behavioral, physiological and spiritual reactions. Find a trusted friend to talk to about your experience. Remember to keep in confidence what people shared with you. Talk about your reactions to the experience. Sharing the experience will help you to assimilate what has occurred.

- Realize that repetitive thoughts and sleep difficulties are normal reactions. Do not fight the sleep difficulty, this will usually pass in a few days. Try the following. Eliminate caffeine for four hours prior to your bedtime, create the best sleep environment you can, consider taking a few moments before turning out the lights to write down your thoughts, thus emptying your mind. Try reading or listening to peaceful music.

- Avoid excessive media exposure, particularly during highly-publicized tragedies. This was certainly a problem in the wake of the September 11th. Take time to get away from the action.

- Give yourself permission to rest, relax and engage in some non-threatening activity. Engage in physical exercise to dissipate the stress energy that has been generated.

- The result of exposure to a traumatic event may create a desire to isolate and withdraw, creating a strain on the spouse and significant others. Remember that they have no way of knowing why you have closed down and pulled away— leaving them to imagine the worst regarding your relationship. In order to maintain your physical, emotional and mental relationship intimacy, communication must continue. Explain to your partner that you need some space, letting them know this need is not about them. Rather, it is related to the traumatic event you have experienced. Set time aside to talk about the incident, thus allowing your partner to be a part of this difficult time. Share with them your needs—they cannot read your mind. Plan time together doing things you enjoy. Stay connected.

- Spend time with your family and friends; stay connected with them. Resist the urge to retreat into your own world. You need their support following an emotionally-charged event.

- Create a journal. Writing about traumatic experiences is helpful in exposing ourselves to painful thoughts and feelings, and in helping us to assimilate these experiences.

- If necessary, seek the assistance of a professional. If you find that the experience is powerful and is staying with you for an extended period of time, allow yourself the advantage of professional support and education. Remember that you are a normal person who has experienced an abnormal event.

- Seek spiritual guidance (e.g., clergy) if there is a desire to facilitate your emotional and spiritual strength. Traumatic events may cause doubt in one's faith and thus, a crisis event may be an opportunity to reaffirm your belief.

- Have the strength to let go. It requires courage to face the powerful emotions within you.

Conclusion

In our efforts to help others during traumatic events, we can fall prey to traumatic stress. It is critical that we recognize when it is appropriate for us to intervene with others and when we should leave this responsibility to another caregiver. If we do elect to provide support to others, we must always remember to take care of ourselves.

CHAPTER EIGHT

Conclusion

Acute Traumatic Stress Management (ATSM) was developed to raise the level of care beyond traditional emergency medical intervention. Unlike crisis intervention that typically focuses on "psychological first-aid" in the aftermath of a tragedy, ATSM offers practical strategies to address the emergent psychological needs of individuals *during* traumatic exposure.

ATSM has served as a *Traumatic Stress Response Protocol* by helping emergency responders to recognize the earliest signs of traumatic stress— and empower them with practical intervention strategies. By reaching people early with ATSM, we have prevented acute traumatic stress reactions from becoming chronic stress disorders.

Comprehensive Acute Traumatic Stress Management (CATSM) reflects the expansion of the ATSM model by addressing the emergent psychological needs of individuals, groups and organizations before, during and after a traumatic event. CATSM is a *Traumatic Stress Response Protocol* for *all* people who endeavor to help others during times of crisis.

Caregivers frequently encounter individuals who exhibit a vast array of traumatic stress reactions—from complete withdrawal to a cascade of overwhelming emotion. The ATSM process incorporates practical techniques for breaking through these emotional states—enabling us to engage particularly challenging individuals.

ATSM provides "practical tools" for addressing the wide spectrum of traumatic experiences—from mild to the most severe. It is a goal-directed process delivered within the framework of a facilitative or helping attitudinal climate. ATSM aims to "jump-start" an individual's coping and problem-solving abilities. It seeks to stabilize acute symptoms of traumatic stress and stimulate healthy, adaptive functioning. Finally, ATSM may increase the likelihood of an individual pursuing mental health intervention, if need be, in the future.

ATSM offers a preconceived plan for addressing the disorganization and unpredictability of a traumatic event. Notwithstanding, ATSM helps us to understand and appreciate the variability in individuals' reactions during traumatic exposure—that responses may not fall neatly into *any* preconceived plan. Consequently, like a yachtsman who has to adjust his sails to the rapidly shifting patterns of the wind, we will have to adjust our approaches to address the unique psychological experiences of those we serve.

We know that people who are exposed to trauma experience the "Imprint of Horror"—the sights, sounds and smells recorded in one's mind during a traumatic event. These perceptions often precipitate acute traumatic stress reactions and chronic stress disorders. In the same way that these negative stimuli can be etched in peoples' minds during traumatic exposure—a period of heightened suggestibility and vulnerability, so too may the positive, adaptive forces of ATSM (e.g., active listening, empathic understanding, a supportive presence, etc.).

ATSM may be sufficient, in and of itself, in addressing the emergent psychological needs of individuals who have been exposed to traumatic events. Or, it may serve as the beginning of a lifelong process of helping victims to become survivors and, ultimately, thrivers.

BIBLIOGRAPHY

American Foundation for Suicide Prevention (1996). Suicide Facts: Child and Adolescent Suicide.

American Psychiatric Association (1994). Diagnostic and statistical manual of mental disorders (4th ed.) Washington, DC: Author.

American Psychological Association (1999). Warning signs. http://helping.apa.org.

Baker, J.E., & Sedney, M. (1996). How bereaved children cope with loss: An overview. In C.A. Corr & D.M. Corr (Eds.), Handbook of childhood death and bereavement (pp. 109-129). New York: Springer.

Belkin, G.S. (1988). Introduction to counseling. Dubugue, Ia: Wm.C.Brown.

Blancharg, E.B., & Hickling, E.J. (1997). After the crash: Assessment and treatment of motor vehicle accident survivors. Washington, DC: American Psychological Association.

Bolton, R. (1979). People skills. New York: Simon & Schuster.

Bourne, E.J. (1990) The anxiety & phobia workbook. Oakland, CA: New Harbinger.

Bowlby, J. (1969). Attachment. New York: Basic Books.

Bowlby, J. (1980). Attachment and loss, Vol. 3 - Sadness and depression. New York: Basic Books.

Brom, D., Kleber, R. & Hofman, M. (1993). Victims of traffic accidents: Incidence and prevention of post-traumatic stress disorder. Journal of Clinical Psychology, (pp. 49, 131-139).

Callahan, J. (1998). Crisis theory and crisis intervention in emergencies. In P. Klesspies (Ed.). Emergencies in Mental Health Practice (pp.22-40). New York: Guilford.

Caplan, G. (1964). Principles of preventive psychiatry. New York: Basic Books

Davidson, L.E. (1989). Suicide cluster and youth. In C.R. Pfeffer (Ed.), Suicide among youth (pp. 83-99). Washington, DC: American Psychiatric Press.

Dunne, E.J., McIntosh, J.L., & Dunne-Maxim, K. , Editors. (1987). Suicide and its aftermath. New York: W.W. Norton.

Dutton, M.S. (1994). Post-traumatic therapy with domestic violence survivors. In M.D. Williams & J.F. Sommer (Eds.), Handbook of post-traumatic therapy (pp. 146-161). Westport, CT: Greenwood Press.

Everly, G.S. (1993). Psychotraumatology: A two-factor formulation of posttraumatic stress. Integrative physiology and behavioral science, (pp. 28, 270-278).

Everly, G.S. (1995). Innovations in disaster and trauma psychology, volume one: applications in emergency services and disaster response. Ellicott City, MD: Chevron.

Everly, G.S., Flannery, R.B., & Mitchell, J. (1999). Critical Incident Stress Management: A review of literature. Aggression and violent behavior: a review journal.

Everly, G.S., Jr., & Mitchell, J.T. (1999). Critical incident stress management. Ellicott City, MD: Chevron.

Figley, C.R. (1995). Compassion fatigue: coping with secondary traumatic stress disorder in those who treat the traumatized. New York: Brunner/Mazel.

Foy, D.W. (1992). Introduction and description of the disorder. In D.W. Foy (Ed.), Treating PTSD: cognitive-behavioral strategies (pp 1-12). New York: Guilford.

Fremouw, W.J., de Perczel, M., & Ellis, T.E. (1990). Suicide risk: Assessment and response guidelines. New York: Pergamon.

Golan, N. (1978). Treatment in crisis situations. New York: The Free Press.

Greenstone, J.L., & Levittown, S.C. (1993). Elements of crisis intervention: Crises & how to respond to them. California: Brooks/Cole.

Harvey, J.H. (2000). Give sorrow words. Philadelphia: Taylor & Francis Group.

Harvey, J.H. & E.D. Miller (2000). Loss and trauma. Philadelphia: Taylor & Francis Group.

Hill, D.C., & Foster, Y.M. (1996). Postvention with early and middle adolescents. In C.A. Corr & D.E. Balk (Eds.), Handbook of adolescent death and bereavement (pp. 250-272). New York: Springer.

Kaplan, H.I., Sadock, B.J. & Grebb, J.A. (1994). Synopsis of psychiatry. Baltimore, MD: Williams & Wilkins.

Kates, A.R. (1999). Copshock: surviving posttraumatic stress disorder. Tuscon, AZ: Holbrook Street Press.

Kirschenbaum, H. & Henderson, V. L., Editors (1989). The Carl Rogers reader. Boston: Houghton Mifflin Company.

Kubler-Ross, E. (1969). On death and dying. New York: MacMillan.

Kurke, M.I., & Scrivner, E.M., Editors. (1995). Police psychology into the 21st century. Hillsdale, NJ: Lawrence Erlbaum Associates.

Lerner, M. (1988). Perceptions of desirable characteristics of psychotherapists. Doctoral Dissertation. Hofstra University.

Lerner, M. (1997). Early Intervention–A Multidisciplinary Effort. Trauma Response. The American Academy of Experts in Traumatic Stress, Winter, 1997.

Lerner, M. (1998). From the President's Desk. Trauma Response. The American Academy of Experts in Traumatic Stress.

Lerner, M. (2004). Surviving and Thriving: Living Through a Traumatic Experience. www.DrMarkLerner.com.

Limmer, D., O'Keefe, M., Grant, H., Murray, R., Bergeron, D., (2001). Emergency Care, Ninth Edition. Upper Saddle River, NJ: Brady.

Martin, D.G. (1983). Counseling and therapy skills. Prospect Heights, IL: Waveland Press.

Matsakis, A. (1996). I can't get over it: A handbook for trauma survivors (2nd ed.). Oakland, CA: New Harbinger Publications.

Meek, C.L. (Ed.) (1990). Posttraumatic stress disorder: assessment differential diagnosis and forensic evaluation. Sarasota, FL: Professional Resource Exchange, Inc.

Meichenbaum, D. (1994). A clinical handbook/practical therapist manual for assessing and treating adults with post-traumatic stress disorder. Ontario, Canada: Institute Press.

Meyers, A.W., & Craighead, W.D. (1984) (Eds.). Cognitive behavior therapy with children. New York: Plenum Press.

Mitchell, J.T. (1983a). When disaster strikes... The critical incident stress debriefing process. Journal of emergency medical services, (pp. 8, [1], 36-39).

Mitchell, J.T. & Everly, G. (1996). Critical incident stress debriefing: an operations manual for the prevention of traumatic stress among emergency services and disaster workers. Ellicott City, MD: Chevron Publishing Corporation.

Mitchell, J.T. & Everly, G.S. (1997). Scientific evidence for Critical Incident Stress Management. Journal of Emergency Medical Services, (pp. 22, 87-93).

Mitchell, J.T. & Everly, G.S., Jr. (1997). Critical incident stress debriefing. Ellicott City, MD: Chevron Publishing Corporation.

Mitchell, J.T., & Resnick, H.L.P. (1986). Emergency response to crisis. Ellicott City, MD: Chevron Publishing Corporation.

Myers, D. (1995). Worker stress during long-term disaster recovery efforts. In G.S. Everly (Ed.) Innovations in disaster and trauma psychology, volume one (pp. 158-191). Ellicott City, MD: Chevron Publishing Corporation.

Myers, D., & Wee, D. F. (2005). Disaster Mental Health Services. Brunner-Routledge.

Olweus, D. (1984). Development of stable aggressive reaction: Patterns on males. In R.J. Blanchard & D.C. Blanchard (Eds.), Advances in the study of aggression (pp. 103-137). New York: Academic Press.

Range, L. (1996). Suicide and life-threatening behavior in childhood. In C.A. Corr & D.E. Balk (Eds.), Handbook of adolescent death and bereavement (pp. 71-88). New York: Springer.

Rogers, C. (1951). Client-centered therapy. Boston: Houghton Mifflin.

Schaefer, D. & Lyons (1993). How do we tell the children. New York: Newmarket Press.

Schiraldi, G. R. (2000) The Post-Traumatic Stress Disorder Sourcebook. Lowell House.

Scott, M.J., & Stradling, S.G. (1992). Counselling for posttraumatic stress disorder. London: Sage.

Shelton, R., & Kelly, J. (1995). EMS Stress: An emergency responder's handbook for living well. Carlsbad, CA: Mosby.

Simon, R.I. (Ed.). (1995). Posttraumatic stress disorder in litigation. Washington, DC: American Psychiatric Press.

Solomon, R., (1995). Critical incident stress management in law enforcement. In G.S. Everly (Ed.) Innovations in disaster and trauma psychology, volume 1 (pp. 123-157). Ellicott City, MD: Chevron Publishing Corporation.

Solomon, S., Gerrity, E.T., & Muff, A.M. (1992). Efficacy of treatments of Posttraumatic Stress Disorder: An empirical review. Journal of the American Medical Association, 268, 633-638.

Terr, L. (1991). Childhood trauma: An outline and overview. American journal of psychiatry, 148, 10-20.

Ursano, R.J., McCaughey, B.GF., & Fullerton, C.S. (1994). Individual and community responses to trauma and disaster: The structure of human chaos. New York: Cambridge.

Weaver, J.D. (1995). Disasters: mental health interventions. Sarasota, FL: Professional Resource Press.

Williams, M.B. & Sommer, J.F., Jr. (1994). Handbook of posttraumatic therapy. Westport CT: Greenwood Press.

APPENDICES

The Appendices Section of this publication offers a number of practical documents that may be utilized by *all* caregivers. These documents are part of a large collection of *Trauma Response® Infosheets™* published by The American Academy of Experts in Traumatic Stress.

The following *Infosheets* have been derived from information offered in this publication and are provided as a public service by the Academy. Please feel at liberty to reproduce these handouts in their original form. Appropriate documents may be offered to victims "at the scene" of tragedies, provided as supplementary information for educational training programs and workshops, utilized to review material offered in this publication, etc.:

A.   The 10 Stages of Acute Traumatic Stress Management:
       A Brief Summary

B.   How Do People Respond During Traumatic Exposure?

C.   Helpful Information During and After a Traumatic Event

D.   What Specific Strategies May Be Utilized to Connect with
       Particularly Challenging, Emotionally Distraught,
       Individuals?

E.   Indicators Suggestive of a Greater Likelihood of
       Self-Destructive Potential

F.   "High-risk" Indicators for Posttraumatic Stress Disorder (PTSD)

G.   How Can We Help Grieving Individuals?

H.   "The ATSM Field Pack"
       Items Utilized in the Field for the Provision of ATSM

Trauma Response®

PRODUCED AS A PUBLIC SERVICE OF
THE AMERICAN ACADEMY OF EXPERTS IN TRAUMATIC STRESS, INC.
368 VETERANS MEMORIAL HIGHWAY, COMMACK, NEW YORK 11725
TEL. (631) 543-2217 • FAX (631) 543-6977
WWW.ATSM.ORG • WWW.TRAUMATIC-STRESS.ORG • WWW.AAETS.ORG

Infosheet™

The 10 Stages of Acute Traumatic Stress Management (ATSM):
A Brief Summary

Reprinted from *Comprehensive Acute Traumatic Stress Management*™
by Mark D. Lerner, Ph.D. and Raymond D. Shelton, Ph.D.
© 2005 by The American Academy of Experts in Traumatic Stress, Inc.

1. **Assess for Danger/Safety for Self and Others**
   - Are there factors that can compromise your safety or the safety of others?

2. **Consider the Mechanism of Injury**
   - How did the event physically and perceptually impact upon the individual?

3. **Evaluate the Level of Responsiveness**
   - Is individual alert and responsive? Under the influence of a substance?

4. **Address Medical Needs**
   - For those who are specifically trained to manage acute medical conditions

5. **Observe & Identify**
   - Who has been exposed to the event and who is evidencing signs of traumatic stress?

6. **Connect with the Individual**
   - Introduce yourself, state your title and/or position. Once he is medically evaluated, move the individual away from the stressor. Begin to develop rapport.

7. **Ground the Individual**
   - Discuss the facts, assure safety if he is, have him "Tell his story." Discuss behavioral and physiological responses.

8. **Provide Support**
   - Be empathic. Communicate a desire to understand the feelings that lie behind his words.

9. **Normalize the Response**
   - Normalize, validate and educate.... "*Normal* person trying to cope with an *abnormal* event."

10. **Prepare for the Future**
    - Review the event, bring the person to the present, describe events in the future and provide referrals.

PRODUCED AS A PUBLIC SERVICE OF
THE AMERICAN ACADEMY OF EXPERTS IN TRAUMATIC STRESS, INC.
368 VETERANS MEMORIAL HIGHWAY, COMMACK, NEW YORK 11725
TEL. (631) 543-2217 • FAX (631) 543-6977
WWW.ATSM.ORG • WWW.TRAUMATIC-STRESS.ORG • WWW.AAETS.ORG

How Do People Respond *During* Traumatic Exposure?

Reprinted from *Comprehensive Acute Traumatic Stress Management*™
by Mark D. Lerner, Ph.D. and Raymond D. Shelton, Ph.D.
© 2005 by The American Academy of Experts in Traumatic Stress, Inc.

The following emotional, cognitive, behavioral, physiological and spiritual reactions are often experienced by people *during* a traumatic event. It is important to recognize that these reactions do not necessarily represent an unhealthy or maladaptive response. Rather, they may be viewed as *normal* responses to an *abnormal* event. When these reactions are experienced in the future (i.e., weeks, months or even years after the event), are joined by other symptoms (e.g., recurrent distressing dreams, "flashbacks," avoidance behaviors, etc.), and interfere with social, occupational or other important areas of functioning, a psychiatric disorder may be in evidence. These individuals should pursue help with a mental health professional.

Emotional Responses during a traumatic event may include *shock,* in which the individual may present a highly anxious, active response or perhaps a seemingly stunned, emotionally-numb response. He may describe feeling as though he is "in a fog." He may exhibit *denial*, in which there is an inability to acknowledge the impact of the situation or perhaps, that the situation has occurred. He may evidence *dissociation*, in which he may seem dazed and apathetic, and he may express feelings of unreality. Other frequently observed acute emotional responses may include panic, fear, intense feelings of aloneness, hopelessness, helplessness, emptiness, uncertainty, horror, terror, anger, hostility, irritability, depression, grief and feelings of guilt.

Cognitive Responses to traumatic exposure are often reflected in impaired concentration, confusion, disorientation, difficulty in making a decision, a short attention span, suggestibility, vulnerability, forgetfulness, self-blame, blaming others, lowered self-efficacy, thoughts of losing control, hypervigilance, and perseverative thoughts of the traumatic event. For example, upon extrication of a survivor from an automobile accident, he may cognitively still "be in" the automobile "playing the tape" of the accident over and over in his mind.

Behavioral Responses in the face of a traumatic event may include withdrawal, "spacing-out," non-communication, changes in speech patterns, regressive behaviors, erratic movements, impulsivity, a reluctance to abandon property, seemingly aimless walking, pacing, an inability to sit still, an exaggerated startle response and antisocial behaviors.

Physiological Responses may include rapid heart beat, elevated blood pressure, difficulty breathing*, shock symptoms*, chest pains*, cardiac palpitations*, muscle tension and pains, fatigue, fainting, flushed face, pale appearance, chills, cold clammy skin, increased sweating, thirst, dizziness, vertigo, hyperventilation, headaches, grinding of teeth, twitches and gastrointestinal upset.

Require immediate medical evaluation

Spiritual Responses to a traumatic incident often include anger and a distance from God. There may be a withdrawal from attending religious services. Sometimes the opposite of these reactions is experienced with a sudden turn toward God and uncharacteristic involvement in religious community activity. Additional reactions may include faith practice (e.g., prayers, scriptures, hymns, worship, communion), as empty and without meaning. There is often a belief that God is powerless, doesn't care or has failed to protect creating a questioning of one's basic beliefs. There is often anger at clergy.

𝕿rauma 𝕽esponse®

PRODUCED AS A PUBLIC SERVICE OF
THE AMERICAN ACADEMY OF EXPERTS IN TRAUMATIC STRESS, INC.
368 VETERANS MEMORIAL HIGHWAY, COMMACK, NEW YORK 11725
TEL. (631) 543-2217 • FAX (631) 543-6977
WWW.ATSM.ORG • WWW.TRAUMATIC-STRESS.ORG • WWW.AAETS.ORG

Helpful Information During and After a Traumatic Event

Reprinted from *Comprehensive Acute Traumatic Stress Management*™
by Mark D. Lerner, Ph.D. and Raymond D. Shelton, Ph.D.
© 2005 by The American Academy of Experts in Traumatic Stress, Inc.

Immediate Traumatic Incident Stress Management:

- Avoid the use of alcohol and caffeine. Alcohol is a depressant and as such will intensify the negative reactions experienced following the incident. Caffeine will increase anxiety and negatively impact the ability to sleep.

- Drink plenty of fluids such as water or juice. Avoid consuming large quantities of soda that contains caffeine.

- Use quick relaxation techniques to regain control of emotions. Take a slow deep breath by inhaling through the nose, holding the breath for 3 seconds and exhaling through the mouth. Upon exhalation the words "relax," "let go," " I can handle this" may be spoken. Repeat the process a second time. Utilize this technique when you become aware of negative reactions or thoughts beginning to occur.

- Become physically comfortable. While the incident may not be under control, you can take back small pieces of control by taking simple action steps. Wash your face, hands, replace wet clothing, and step outside for a breath of fresh air and a change of scene. These simple acts will bring a small level of control to an out of control situation. Repeat them as often as necessary throughout the incident engagement.

Stress Management following disengagement from incident:

- Resist the desire to withdraw and isolate. Maintaining a connection with the people in your life is of the utmost importance. Maintain your support systems of family and friends. If you feel the need for some quiet time, tell those around you of this need. Ask them to give you some "space." Do not just shut down.

- Engage in simple exercise. The stress reactions produced by the incident, coupled by the wide range of thoughts, will produce a sense of unrest. Engaging in simple exercise such as walking, biking, and swimming will assist in dissipating these reactions.

- Limit exposure to the news. We live in a media powerful world that allows us to experience events in real time. The constant exposure to the incident through media will continue to trigger negative reactions as the event unfolds over and over. Choose a news program to stay informed. Watch the program in the early evening and allow yourself time to process the information and take appropriate action steps to alleviate the stress reaction that may be created. Do not watch the news immediately prior to going to bed.

- Maintain a normal schedule. Traumatic incidents disrupt the sense of normalcy. By maintaining as normal a schedule as possible you protect some degree of a normal existence while in the midst of the incident. During this time of stress it is important to continue to do things you enjoy. Schedule time for recreational activity. Go ahead and play your golf game—but don't worry about winning, just have fun. Make daily decisions and follow through.

- Set short range goals. Goals provide a sense of direction during a time when confusion and fear of the unknown are present. Attempt to set goals for 1 week, 2 weeks, etc. Be certain that the goal you set is realistic and manageable. By setting realistic goals you will avoid the frustration that always accompanies failed goals.

- Set limits for yourself. Avoid the urge to push on without allowing sufficient time to relax and unwind. Give yourself permission to take the "intermission." Listen to the "wisdom" of your body. When you are tired... rest.

- Be aware of your feelings and talk about them. Keep a journal and write your thoughts. If you have difficulty sleeping, do not fight the sleeplessness. Find a quiet place and write your way through the sleepless nights. The process of talking or writing will assist you in quieting your mind thus enabling you to relax and sleep.

- During the time period immediately following a traumatic incident realize that those around you are also in varying levels of distress. Be tolerant, seek first to understand others' reactions and allow them space.

- Resist the desire to make major life changes. Allow time for the incident to pass and recovery to occur before making major decisions.

- Eat well balanced meals.

- Remember your symptoms are normal having experienced a powerful negative event. Understand that during times of great distress "it is OK not to be OK."

- Seek professional assistance if your symptoms persist.

Guidelines for assisting children:

- Help yourself first. Be certain you are in a good frame of mind when discussing the incident.

- Be honest and open discussing the incident in age appropriate terms.

- Encourage talk about the event.

- Children may not communicate their feelings with words. Encourage them to draw a picture.

- Acknowledge that being frightened is OK.

- Monitor and limit media exposure. Allow time for discussion following exposure to powerful media stimuli.

- Spend extra time at bedtime.

- Remain connected, tune in to their needs.

- Be tolerant during times of distress.

- Hug and cuddle with young children.

Trauma Response®

PRODUCED AS A PUBLIC SERVICE OF
THE AMERICAN ACADEMY OF EXPERTS IN TRAUMATIC STRESS, INC.
368 VETERANS MEMORIAL HIGHWAY, COMMACK, NEW YORK 11725
TEL. (631) 543-2217 • FAX (631) 543-6977
WWW.ATSM.ORG • WWW.TRAUMATIC-STRESS.ORG • WWW.AAETS.ORG

What Specific Strategies May Be Utilized to Connect with Particularly Challenging, Emotionally Distraught, Individuals?

Reprinted from *Comprehensive Acute Traumatic Stress Management*™
by Mark D. Lerner, Ph.D. and Raymond D. Shelton, Ph.D.
© 2005 by The American Academy of Experts in Traumatic Stress, Inc.

During traumatic exposure, individual reactions may present on a continuum from a totally detached, withdrawn reaction to the most intense displays of emotion (e.g., uncontrollable crying, screaming, panic, anger, fear, etc.). These situations present a considerable challenge. In order to address an individual's emergent psychological needs, you must "break through" these emotional states.

As described previously, be sure to address the initial stages of ATSM (i.e., emergency medical protocol) prior to attempts at connecting with the challenging individual. Following, are five highly practical techniques that you may utilize to engage these individuals. These strategies may be referred to as the "Five D's"—1) Distraction, 2) Disruption, 3) Diffusion. 4) Decision, and 5) Direction.

1. Distraction

This technique aims to distract and refocus the challenging individual. The approach may be likened to a strategy that is often used by parents of young children. When the child shows interest in the TV remote control, the parent distracts the child with a "transitional object"—a more appropriate, yet interesting toy. In the same way, when an individual is unresponsive to efforts to engage, or possibly at the other end of the continuum crying uncontrollably, you may distract and refocus the individual. Introduce an irrelevant ,yet highly interesting topic. The more concise and thought-provoking the topic is, the better. Consider the following example:

(continued)

An emergency medical service supervisor raced to the scene of a child who was reportedly choking. When he arrived at the scene, a paramedic was walking the girl out the front door of a home toward the waiting ambulance. The medic reported to his supervisor that the child had a small piece of chicken bone lodged in her soft pallet. The child was teary-eyed and coughing gently—as if to clear her throat. Following the child out the door were a number of young siblings and family friends. They were crying uncontrollably and seemed to be "feeding off" each other's level of hysteria. The EMS supervisor walked over to the children and said, "I feel so sorry for you guys!" He immediately caught their attention. He then followed with, "You're all going to have to go to your piggy banks to get some money to buy ice cream for your friend—she's going to have a sore throat when she comes home later." The children's reactions quickly, almost magically, shifted to laughing. Having the kids engaged, he then lowered himself to one knee and gave them a chance to "tell their story" of how scary it was seeing their friend choking and to review the facts of the event. Following the ATSM model, he then supported them, normalized their reactions and prepared them for her return home.

The key to this Distraction Technique is that the topic that is introduced, or the comment that is made, is sufficiently powerful to distract and divert the individual's attention. Be careful not to say something that implies a lack of concern. Also, make sure that you subsequently return to the reality of the situation by discussing the event at a factual level.

2. Disruption

A second strategy that may be utilized with challenging individuals involves a powerful disruption of the emotional reaction. First, come down to the person's level, either kneeling or sitting, and establish eye contact. In a clear and calm voice, while looking directly into the individual's eyes, give a basic command using his/her name: "Mary, I want you to take a deep breath." Then pause, and in a slightly louder more forceful voice, repeat the command exactly as stated: "Mary, I want you to take a deep breath." Continue to repeat the command, always using the same words. Escalate the volume and tone with each command statement. Usually, by the third command the individual will follow your request. At this moment, lower your voice to a calm level and begin to talk. You may instruct the individual to take a second and third slow deep breath. Once you have broken through the emotional state, you will be able to provide direction and support.

Perhaps the greatest advantage of this *Disruption Technique* is that it can be implemented very quickly. Recognize that by utilizing the technique, you will likely be doing something very different from others. For example, your focus on the individual's breathing may disrupt a seemingly ineffective cycle of effort, by others, to gain control over hysterical behavior.

3. *Diffusion*

A third strategy for connecting with the challenging individual involves diffusion of the emotional state. For example, you may begin your conversation with an anxious or possibly agitated individual at a voice rate and tone comparable to his. If he is speaking loudly, increase your volume to match his. If he is speaking rapidly, speak rapidly. If you are required to move around with the individual, match his pace. Gradually, begin to slow the physical pace, lower the volume of your voice and slow your rate of speech. As the individual begins to respond in a calm, more controlled manner, provide direction and support. Move him away from the scene, have him take a deep breath and continue with the ATSM process.

Interestingly, this technique may also be utilized in the opposite direction. For example, with a seemingly depressed or generally non-communicative individual, begin your conversation with the individual at a voice rate and tone comparable to his. If he is speaking softly, decrease your volume to match his. If he is speaking slowly, speak slowly. If you are required to move around with the individual, match his pace. Gradually, begin to increase the physical pace, raise the volume of your voice and increase your rate of speech. As the individual begins to respond in a more energetic, involved manner, provide direction and support. Move him away from the scene, have him take a deep breath and continue with the ATSM process.

4. *Decision*

A fourth strategy, often effective in dealing with a challenging individual, involves having the victim make a decision. Being asked to decide between two basic choices often distracts the challenging individual and focuses him on adaptive, constructive behavior. It gives an individual who is feeling out-of-control during a crisis the ability to regain a sense of control through his decision-making. Consider the following:

After learning that her co-worker had suffered a sudden heart attack and died the night before, a young employee, Jennifer, sat at her desk crying hysterically. She was inconsolable. When Jennifer was asked if she would like to take a walk to the ladies lounge on the South side of the third floor, or sit in the atrium under the new palm trees, she chose the latter. This decision, involving some detailed choices, diverted Jennifer's attention and "short-circuited" her thinking. Once in the atrium, efforts to connect with Jennifer were more effective.

5. Direction

As indicated previously, particularly when time is limited, providing clear authoritative direction is often an effective vehicle for gaining rapid control. The challenging individual who remains non-responsive to a warm and supportive effort to connect may respond to firm direction. Consider this example:

After hearing reports of a teenage boy disappearing under a wave while buggy-boarding, lifeguards found themselves wrestling with two agitated boys who were racing into the ocean to find him. A strong undertow was compromising their safety. A senior lifeguard called for immediate assistance. One lifeguard remained with the boys, speaking calmly with them—trying to engage them. This approach only seemed to escalate the boys' agitation and even, rage. A park police officer arrived at the scene, sized-up the event, and immediately directed the boys in a loud, stern voice to, "take a seat" on their boards. In this case, the police officer was able to gain rapid control and begin a constructive process of fact-finding by utilizing authoritative direction.

When considering the utilization of Distraction, Disruption, Diffusion, Decision or Direction, realize that the nature of the event, time variables and individuals' responses will influence your approach. For example, the Diffusion technique, by its very nature, will take more time to implement than the Distraction, Disruption, Decision or Direction techniques. Notwithstanding, it may be the best choice given a particular situation.

The "Five D's" are practical intervention techniques. However, they *must* be practiced. Breaking through strong emotional reactions *during* a traumatic event will require a confident, well-rehearsed approach. Having strong familiarity with these strategies will enable you to apply them with the most challenging individuals.

Trauma Response®

PRODUCED AS A PUBLIC SERVICE OF
THE AMERICAN ACADEMY OF EXPERTS IN TRAUMATIC STRESS, INC.
368 VETERANS MEMORIAL HIGHWAY, COMMACK, NEW YORK 11725
TEL. (631) 543-2217 • FAX (631) 543-6977
WWW.ATSM.ORG • WWW.TRAUMATIC-STRESS.ORG • WWW.AAETS.ORG

Indicators Suggestive of a Greater Likelihood of Self-Destructive Potential

Reprinted from *Comprehensive Acute Traumatic Stress Management*™
by Mark D. Lerner, Ph.D. and Raymond D. Shelton, Ph.D.
© 2005 by The American Academy of Experts in Traumatic Stress, Inc.

- has previously attempted suicide

- has a history of self-destructive behavior

- is talking or writing about suicide

- has a specific plan

- has access to a gun or other lethal means

- has harmed others

- is suffering from depression or other mental illness

- has experienced a prior tragedy (e.g., suicide of family member)

- is involved with alcohol and/or other substance

- has harmed animals

- describes his situation as "hopeless"

- has sleep and/or eating disturbances

- is talking about "not being around...", saying good-bye

- gives away possessions

𝔗𝔯𝔞𝔲𝔪𝔞 𝔕𝔢𝔰𝔭𝔬𝔫𝔰𝔢®

Infosheet™

PRODUCED AS A PUBLIC SERVICE OF
THE AMERICAN ACADEMY OF EXPERTS IN TRAUMATIC STRESS, INC.
368 VETERANS MEMORIAL HIGHWAY, COMMACK, NEW YORK 11725
TEL. (631) 543-2217 • FAX (631) 543-6977
WWW.ATSM.ORG • WWW.TRAUMATIC-STRESS.ORG • WWW.AAETS.ORG

"High-risk" indicators for Posttraumatic Stress Disorder (PTSD)

Reprinted from *Comprehensive Acute Traumatic Stress Management*™
by Mark D. Lerner, Ph.D. and Raymond D. Shelton, Ph.D.
© 2005 by The American Academy of Experts in Traumatic Stress, Inc.

- prior exposure to severe adverse life events (e.g., combat)

- prior victimization (e.g., childhood sexual and physical abuse)

- significant losses

- exposure to a *severe* event

- close proximity to the event

- extended exposure to danger

- pre-trauma anxiety and depression

- chronic medical condition

- substance involvement

- history of trouble with authority (e.g., stealing, vandalism, etc.)

- mental illness

- lack of familial/social support

- having no opportunity to vent (i.e., unable to tell one's story)

- strong emotional reactions upon exposure to the event

- physically injured by event, etc.

𝕿𝖗𝖆𝖚𝖒𝖆 𝕽𝖊𝖘𝖕𝖔𝖓𝖘𝖊®

PRODUCED AS A PUBLIC SERVICE OF
THE AMERICAN ACADEMY OF EXPERTS IN TRAUMATIC STRESS, INC.
368 VETERANS MEMORIAL HIGHWAY, COMMACK, NEW YORK 11725
TEL. (631) 543-2217 • FAX (631) 543-6977
WWW.ATSM.ORG • WWW.TRAUMATIC-STRESS.ORG • WWW.AAETS.ORG

How Can We Help Grieving Individuals?

Reprinted from *Comprehensive Acute Traumatic Stress Management*™
by Mark D. Lerner, Ph.D. and Raymond D. Shelton, Ph.D.
© 2005 by The American Academy of Experts in Traumatic Stress, Inc.

Grief refers to the feelings that are precipitated by loss. The early reactions that we see in grieving individuals occur during a period of "Numbing." Initially, the individual may present in shock. There may be a highly anxious, active response with an outburst of extremely intense distress or perhaps a seemingly stunned, emotionally-numb response.

During this early phase, you may likely observe denial—an inability to acknowledge the impact of the event or perhaps, that the event has occurred. The individual may evidence dissociation, in which he may seem dazed and apathetic, and he may express feelings of unreality. It is not unusual for people to make statements such as, "I can't believe it," "This is not happening," "This has got to be a bad dream," etc. Finally, there may be periods of intense emotion (e.g., crying, screaming, rage, anger, fear, guilt, etc.). Recognize that these kinds of reactions to a traumatic loss are normal responses.

Within hours or perhaps days of the loss, "Yearning and Searching" may be observed. Here, the individual begins to register the reality of the loss. There may be a preoccupation with the lost individual. Symptoms may include, but not be limited to, insomnia, poor appetite, headaches, anxiety, tension, anger, guilt, etc. Sounds and signals may be interpreted as the deceased person's presence.

Within weeks to months following the loss is a period of "Disorganization." Here, feelings of anger and depression are exhibited. The individual may likely pose questions (e.g., "Why did this have to happen?") and evidence periods of "bargaining" (e.g., "If only I could see him just one last time."). Finally, in the months or even years following the loss is a time of "Reorganization." Here, the individual begins to accept the loss-often cultivating new life patterns and goals.

There are no "cookbook" approaches to helping people who are struggling with loss. Perhaps the most important variable is "being there" for the person. Attempt to connect with the him using the ATSM model. Encourage expression of thoughts and feelings without insistence. Recognize that although relatives and friends intend to be supportive, they may be inclined to discourage the expression of feelings-particularly anger and guilt. Avoidance of such expression may prolong the grieving process and can be counterproductive. Allow periods of silence and be careful not to lecture.

When working with grieving individuals, avoid cliches such as "Be strong," and "You're doing so well." Such cliches may only serve to reinforce an individual's feelings of aloneness. Again, allow the bereaved to tell you how they feel and attempt to "normalize" grief reactions. Finally, don't be afraid to touch. A squeeze of the hand, a gentle pat on the back or a warm embrace can show you are there and that you truly care.

Practical Guidelines for Assisting the Grieving Individual

- Provide opportunities for ventilation of emotions.

- Provide support and availability at funeral.

- Practice active and empathic listening (e.g., show acceptance of the feelings and experiences of the griever).

- Provide the individual with an opportunity to reminisce and reflect on their deceased significant other.

- Keep tissues visible and available.

- Encourage the individual to maintain proper care and nurturance for themselves.

- Educate the individual regarding the reactions that they may experience over the next few weeks and/or months (e.g., sleep difficulty, anger, etc.).

- Assist with out-of-work interventions/referrals if indicated. Consider referral to an Employee Assistance Program (EAP).

- Refer for medical consultation in the event of severe insomnia or physical reactions (e.g., migraine headaches).

- Remain mindful for signs that the individual is not coping well (e.g., suicidal threats) and seek medical and/or familial involvement.

- Be mindful of your own feelings surrounding death and know your limitations in your effort to assist the individual.

Trauma Response®

PRODUCED AS A PUBLIC SERVICE OF
THE AMERICAN ACADEMY OF EXPERTS IN TRAUMATIC STRESS, INC.

368 VETERANS MEMORIAL HIGHWAY, COMMACK, NEW YORK 11725
TEL. (631) 543-2217 • FAX (631) 543-6977
WWW.ATSM.ORG • WWW.TRAUMATIC-STRESS.ORG • WWW.AAETS.ORG

"The ATSM Field Pack"
Items Utilized in the Field for the Provision of ATSM

Reprinted from *Comprehensive Acute Traumatic Stress Management*™
by Mark D. Lerner, Ph.D. and Raymond D. Shelton, Ph.D.
© 2005 by The American Academy of Experts in Traumatic Stress, Inc.

We all have "tools of the trade" to perform the requisite functions of our job (e.g., handcuffs, gun, stethoscope, tape, oxygen, fire extinguisher, laptop computer, hand held radio, etc.). Beyond those, there are a number of items that may prove to be helpful (or for some, essential) for those who are addressing the emergent psychological needs of others *during* traumatic exposure. The following list reflects those items that are recommended as part of an "ATSM Field Pack." Some of the items should remain in a vehicle, while others should be carried on your person. Recognize that the magnitude of the event will directly influence the type and number of items that you will need. Consider having the following available:

- A copy of *Comprehensive Acute Traumatic Stress Management*™ (as a reference)
- Copies of *Trauma Response® Infosheets*™ ("handouts" from the back of this publication)
- Referral List (i.e., a list identifying local agencies that may provide further intervention)
- Note Pad and Pen
- Requisite Forms (i.e., as indicated by your profession)
- Photo Identification
- Business Cards
- A Map
- Money (e.g., to purchase food or other necessities)
- Tissues (i.e., preferably a small pack)
- Medication for Yourself (e.g., Antacid, Anti-Diarrheal, Tylenol®, etc.)
- Sunscreen, Insect Repellent, etc. (as indicated)
- Sunglasses

(continued)

- Spare Glasses, Contact Lens Solution, etc.
- Warm Clothing (e.g., including layers, gloves, strong comfortable shoes, etc.)
- Body Armor (i.e., as indicated by the nature of the event and your profession)
- Latex Gloves
- Umbrella
- Flashlight
- Rain Coat and Hat
- Blanket
- Crayons and Paper
- Chewing Gum, Sugar Candy, Snack, etc.
- Bottled Water

The American Academy of Experts in Traumatic Stress

Administrative Offices, 368 Veterans Memorial Highway, Commack, New York 11725
Telephone (631) 543-2217 • Fax (631) 543-6977 • www.atsm.org • www.traumatic-stress.org • www.aaets.org

APPLICATION & EXAMINATION FOR
CERTIFICATION IN ACUTE TRAUMATIC STRESS MANAGEMENT (ATSM)™

This application will be treated as confidential by The American Academy of Experts in Traumatic Stress, Inc. However, applicants who meet the criteria for Certification, and pass the examination, will be identified in *The International Registry of the American Academy of Experts in Traumatic Stress*™, the association's official directory and referral network. The registry is available in bound copy and can also be accessed directly on the Internet at **www.atsm.org** or **www.traumatic-stress.org**

If an applicant is unsuccessful in meeting the criteria for **Certification in Acute Traumatic Stress Management (ATSM)** or passing the examination, the applicant will be informed as to the reason for denial. The applicant will be given a second opportunity to provide additional supportive documentation, if needed, and/or a second opportunity to take the examination (revised version). This application reevaluation and/or reexamination will be offered at no additional charge. Moreover, if an applicant is unsuccessful with the second opportunity, the Academy will refund the full fee required for the application/examination process.

In order for The American Academy of Experts in Traumatic Stress to consider you for Certification, you must be a Member of the Academy in good standing and:

- ❑ complete this application in its entirety,
- ❑ complete the Examination for **Certification in Acute Traumatic Stress Management (ATSM)**,
- ❑ sign the declaration, and
- ❑ enclose one time payment of $225 for review of your application and examination.
  **Please note that your first year Membership dues payment with the Academy will
  be waived and you will be entered as a Member of The American Academy of Experts in Traumatic Stress.**

Enclosed is my check for $_____ or please charge $_____ to my ❑ VISA ❑ American Express ❑ MasterCard ❑ Discover Card

_____   _____   _____   _____
Account No.   Expiration Date   Signature   Date

I. INFORMATION

PLEASE PRINT

Last Name	First Name	M.I.	Title (Dr., Mr., Mrs., Ms.)
Street Address	City	State	Zip Code
Home Telephone	Office Telephone(s)		Fax Number
E-mail Address	Highest Educational Degree		Years of Experience in Field

Profession (e.g., Police Officer, EMS, Firefighter, Nurse, etc.):_____

Area(s) of Interest/Specialization (e.g., Critical Care, Critical Incident Stress Management, Counseling, etc.):

_____

_____

FOR OFFICE USE ONLY: REVIEWER ID. ___ ___ ___   STATUS CODE: ___ ___

PLEASE PHOTOCOPY THIS APPLICATION & EXAMINATION
AND FAX OR MAIL TO THE ACADEMY'S ADMINISTRATIVE OFFICES FOR PROCESSING

	YES	NO
Have your ever been convicted of a felony?	❏	❏
Have you ever been disciplined for any type of unethical or illegal conduct?	❏	❏
Has your professional license/certification ever been revoked, suspended or limited?	❏	❏
Is there action pending to revoke, suspend, or limit your professional license/certification?	❏	❏
Is there any action pending related to your professional practice?	❏	❏
Have you ever voluntarily surrendered your license/certification?	❏	❏
Do you abuse alcohol or other substances?	❏	❏
Have you ever been denied professional liability insurance or has your insurance ever been canceled or denied renewal?	❏	❏

II. EXAMINATION

Carefully place an **X** over your choices from the examination following this page.

1.	a b c d e	11.	a b c d e	21.	a b c d e	31.	a b c d e
2.	a b c d e	12.	a b c d e	22.	a b c d e	32.	a b c d e
3.	a b c d e	13.	a b c d e	23.	a b c d e	33.	a b c d e
4.	a b c d e	14.	a b c d e	24.	a b c d e	34.	a b c d e
5.	a b c d e	15.	a b c d e	25.	a b c d e	35.	a b c d e
6.	a b c d e	16.	a b c d e	26.	a b c d e	36.	a b c d e
7.	a b c d e	17.	a b c d e	27.	a b c d e	37.	a b c d e
8.	a b c d e	18.	a b c d e	28.	a b c d e	38.	a b c d e
9.	a b c d e	19.	a b c d e	29.	a b c d e	39.	a b c d e
10.	a b c d e	20.	a b c d e	30.	a b c d e	40.	a b c d e

III. DECLARATION

As part of the requirements for achieving **Certification in Acute Traumatic Stress Management (ATSM)**, it is necessary that all applicants sign the following statement:

I hereby certify that all information provided in this application packet is accurate and complete. Furthermore, I certify that I personally completed the enclosed **Examination for Certification in Acute Traumatic Stress Management (ATSM)** and that I received no direct assistance from others. I understand that this Certification aims to identify individuals with extensive knowledge of **Acute Traumatic Stress Management (ATSM)**.

I agree to abide by the Academy's Code of Ethical & Professional Standards and agree to hold harmless The American Academy of Experts in Traumatic Stress, Inc. its officers, consultants and employees for any misrepresentation of my credentials and for any malpractice on my part either willful or through negligent conduct, recklessness, and gross misconduct and for all claims, loss, damage, judgment or expense. I understand that The American Academy of Experts in Traumatic Stress does not practice medicine or psychology or provide direct or indirect patient/client care. Furthermore, I understand that **Certification in Acute Traumatic Stress Management (ATSM)** does not attest to my ability to treat survivors of traumatic events.

_____   _____
Signature   Date

PLEASE SELECT THE BEST CHOICE FOR THE FOLLOWING QUESTIONS AND PLACE YOUR ANSWER ON THE PRECEDING PAGE.

1. Which of the following is true concerning Acute Traumatic Stress Management (ATSM)?

   a) It is a goal-directed process delivered within the framework of a *facilitative* or *helping attitudinal climate*.

   b) It aims to "jump-start" an individual's coping and problem-solving abilities.

   c) It seeks to stabilize acute symptoms of traumatic stress and stimulate healthy, adaptive functioning.

   d) It may increase the likelihood of an individual pursuing mental health intervention, if need be, in the future.

   e) all of the above

2. According to the ATSM model, upon arrival at the scene of a traumatic event you should first assess the victim's airway, breathing and circulation.

   a) True

   b) False

3. Which of the following interventions was/were developed specifically to address the emergent psychological needs of individuals *during* traumatic exposure?

   a) "Demobilization"

   b) "Defusings"

   c) Critical Incident Stress Debriefing

   d) Acute Traumatic Stress Management

   e) c and d

4. The implementation of a *Traumatic Stress Response Protocol*, within the framework of well-established emergency response procedures, will better address the needs of the "whole person."

   a) True

   b) False

5. Once you have identified an individual with whom you will implement ATSM, you should

   a) introduce yourself and state your title and/or position.

   b) introduce yourself by name, but avoid using threatening titles and/or positions.

   c) attempt to move the individual away from the stressor if he is medically cleared.

   d) a and c

   e) b and c

6. Which of the following are "high risk" indicators for acute traumatic stress reactions and chronic stress disorders?

   a) the severity of the event itself

   b) substance involvement

   c) history of mental illness

   d) b and c

   e) all of the above

7. Acute Traumatic Stress Management (ATSM) focuses on helping people in the aftermath of a tragedy.

   a) True

   b) False

8. Acute Traumatic Stress Management (ATSM)

   a) was developed primarily for one-on-one interventions

   b) may be applied with several individuals or even a small group of individuals

   c) is a comprehensive crisis response plan

   d) a and b

   e) all of the above

9. When notifying survivors of the death of a family member, the choice of words used to present this information is very important. The appropriate word to use is:

   a) Expired

   b) Past away

   c) Died

   d) Succumbed

   e) all of the above

10. Which of the following is the most acceptable reason for <u>not</u> taking a death notification assignment?

   a) Your lack of experience with making death notifications

   b) Your having experienced a recent significant loss in your life

   c) Your limited training in grief, and traumatic stress reactions

   d) Your limited training in ATSM

   e) None of the above

11. Acute Traumatic Stress Management (ATSM) was developed primarily to address severe traumatic stress reactions.

    a) True

    b) False

12. Acute Traumatic Stress Management (ATSM) is best described as a

    a) comprehensive crisis response plan

    b) multifaceted disaster response plan

    c) practical approach to "psychological first-aid" introduced in the aftermath of a tragedy

    d) critical incident stress debriefing process

    e) none of the above

13. The "Imprint of Horror" refers to

    a) Seeing particularly gruesome events

    b) Hearing people screaming

    c) Smelling burning flesh

    d) Touching an open wound

    e) all of the above

14. If you find yourself feeling emotionally overwhelmed while providing ATSM

    a) it is okay to acknowledge the impact the event is having on you as a human being.

    b) you should make every effort to avoid self-disclosure of specific, personal information.

    c) remind yourself that it is okay not to be okay

    d) a and b

    e) all of the above

15. The ATSM model suggests that there will likely be times when you should address acute traumatic stress reactions prior to addressing medical needs.

    a) True

    b) False

16. "Linking With" another person

    a) is inappropriate and must be avoided at all costs.

    b) is appropriate as long as the event is over and you have the permission of your immediate supervisor.

    c) should be kept between you and the survivor.

    d) refers to the potential to identify personally with the victim.

    e) c and d

17. According to the authors of this publication, intervention during a traumatic event may not necessarily fall neatly into a linear progression of stages. Thus, you should be flexible given the presenting circumstances at hand.

    a) True

    b) False

18. According to *Acute Traumatic Stress Management*, what specific strategies may be utilized to connect with particularly challenging, emotionally distraught, individuals?

    a) Distraction, Disruption, Distension, Decision and Direction

    b) Disruption, Distension, Differentiation, Decision and Direction

    c) Diffusion, Distortion, Distraction, Decision and Direction

    d) Distraction, Disruption, Diffusion, Decision and Direction

    e) none of the above

19. During a traumatic event, confidentiality can rarely be maintained due to the unpredictability of a crisis.

    a) True

    b) False

20. In working with a *young* child who has been exposed to a traumatic event

    a) it is okay to hold and cuddle the child

    b) reassure the child that he is safe—if in fact he is.

    c) separate the child, as quickly as possible, from all stressors—including emotionally overwhelmed adults.

    d) b and c

    e) all of the above

21. The establishment of a *Facilitative* or *Helping Attitudinal Climate* is perhaps most critical during which of the following stages in the ATSM process

    a) Mechanism of Injury Stage

    b) Fact Gathering Stage

    c) Grounding Stage

    d) Connecting Stage

    e) Support Stage

22. During the Observation and Identification Stage, we form an initial impression of the patient and begin to understand the nature of an individual's exposure to a traumatic event.

    a) True

    b) False

23. The ATSM model refers to the "Five Ds." These strategies were developed to evaluate the potential for self-destructive behavior.

   a) True

   b) False

24. During which stage of the ATSM process do we typically focus on the facts surrounding the event?

   a) Mechanism of Injury Stage

   b) Fact Gathering Stage

   c) Grounding Stage

   d) Connecting Stage

   e) Support Stage

25. Reviewing the facts, as well as the individual's behavioral and physiological response, will often stimulate thoughts and feelings.

   a) True

   b) False

26. After addressing medical needs, initiating a connection and beginning a grounding process with a 12 year-old boy who was struck by a car while riding his bicycle, a paramedic moved the youngster to a waiting ambulance. While in the bus, the medic supported the boy while he "told his story," describing his pain as well as his feelings of fear. The medic then gradually began to normalize the boy's experience by suggesting that it would be painful and scary for almost anyone. According to the ATSM model, what would be the next likely step?

   a) Consider the Mechanism of Injury

   b) Develop a *Facilitative* or *Helping Attitudinal Climate*

   c) Assure the child that everything will turn out okay

   d) Prepare the boy for the future

   e) a and d

27. When you become empathic, you may likely become a part of the problem and fall prey to becoming "secondarily victimized" yourself. You will invest considerable energy *experiencing* another person's pain and suffering. You will no longer remain grounded and functional, and your decision-making abilities will likely become clouded.

   a) True

   b) False

28. Which of the following is <u>not</u> an example of an empathic response/statement?

    a) "You seem scared and alone right now."

    b) "It's like you just can't stop playing the tape of the accident over and over in your head."

    c) "I feel so sorry for you. How can I help?"

    d) "Help me understand what you're thinking. It seems like you're frustrated with us."

    e) all of the above

29. Following an automobile accident, a paramedic stated to an injured passenger, "If I'm hearing you correctly, it sounds like the pain is primarily in your right shoulder." This is an example of

    a) an empathic statement

    b) a sympathetic statement

    c) a patronizing statement

    d) a confounding statement

    e) b and d

30. The primary purpose of the "Normalization Stage" is to begin to educate the individual who is experiencing traumatic stress to know that he is not alone, that he is a normal person trying to cope with an abnormal event—that his experience is perhaps his mind's attempt to "make sense of the senseless."

    a) True

    b) False

31. The applicability and efficacy of ATSM may be influenced by a number of critical factors. Which of the following should be considered?

    a) characteristics that are unique to the emergency responder's profession

    b) characteristics of the traumatic event.

    c) characteristics of the individuals that are served

    d) b and c

    e) all of the above

32. The alcohol/substance involved individual presents a challenge to emergency responders. Efforts to implement ATSM will likely be confounded by the influence of the substance itself. It is generally <u>not</u> advisable to

    a) make physical contact

    b) speak in a warm calming tone

    c) avoid loud noises and bright lights

    d) approach the person with another emergency responder standing by

    e) a and d

33. Working with depressed, self-destructive and potentially suicidal individuals presents a challenge for the emergency responder. Which of the following is true?

    a) People who talk about suicide typically do not commit suicide.

    b) You must determine if the individual is truly at-risk of harming himself.

    c) Alcohol and other substances may increase the likelihood of self-destructive behavior.

    d) a and b

    e) none of the above

34. Which of the following is the earliest reaction typically observed in grieving individuals?

    a) Yearning and Searching

    b) Shock

    c) Insomnia

    d) Disorganization

    e) none of the above

35. The "ATSM Field Pack" refers specifically to the

    a) "Tools of the trade" that you should bring when you are called to a traumatic event.

    b) "Tools of the trade" that you should bring when you are called to any event.

    c) items that may prove to be helpful for those who are addressing the emergent psychological needs of others during traumatic exposure.

    d) most essential medical equipment aimed at the preservation of life

    e) none of the above

36. Traumatic stress reactions may lead to Posttraumatic Stress Disorder (PTSD). In these cases, people may experience recurrent and intrusive distressing recollections of the event, distressing dreams, flashbacks, difficulty concentrating, hypervigilance, an exaggerated startle response, and a host of avoidance behaviors.

    a) True

    b) False

37. Which of the following interventions were developed to help people after disengagement from a crisis— following a traumatic experience?

    a) Demobilization and Defusing

    b) Critical Incident Stress Debriefing

    c) Acute Traumatic Stress Management

    d) a and b

    e) b and c

38. Generally, as the severity of a traumatic event increases, so does the level of traumatic stress.

    a) True

    b) False

39. You are assigned to make a death notification to the parents of a teenage boy. After gaining access to the home and making the notification, the mother of the boy begins to scream and cry out his name. She appears to be hyperventilating and out of control. She does not respond to your partner's efforts to calm her. The most appropriate ATSM technique to use in this situation is:

    a) Disruption

    b) Distraction

    c) Diffusion

    d) Disengagement

    e) b and d

40. A *facilitative* or *helping attitudinal climate* is a necessary, and oftentimes sufficient, component in supporting an individual and in mitigating acute traumatic stress reactions during traumatic exposure.

    a) True

    b) False

About The American Academy of Experts in Traumatic Stress®

The American Academy of Experts in Traumatic Stress is a multidisciplinary network of professionals who are committed to the advancement of intervention for survivors of trauma. Our international membership includes individuals from over 200 professions in the health-related fields, emergency services, criminal justice, forensics, law, business and education. The Academy is presently represented by professionals in every state of the United States and over 40 foreign countries.

Society is becoming increasingly aware of the emotional, cognitive, behavioral, physiological and spiritual experience of individuals facing a serious illness or who are exposed to other significant traumatic events. The Academy recognized a need to identify expertise among professionals, across disciplines, and to provide standards for those who regularly work with survivors. Our association is now the largest organization of its kind in the world.

The mission of the Academy is to increase awareness of the effects of trauma and, ultimately, to improve the quality of intervention with survivors. It is in this spirit that we offer:

- Membership/Associate Membership in a prestigious professional association,
- Board Certification Programs,
- Diplomate and Fellow Credentials,
- continuing education credits,
- *Trauma Response®*, *Trauma Response® Infosheets™* and *Trauma Response® E-News,* the official publications of the Academy,
- listing in *The International Registry of The American Academy of Experts in Traumatic Stress™*,
- an award winning "guest quarters" on the Internet at **www.traumatic-stress.org**, **www.aaets.org**, **www.atsm.org**, and **www.schoolcrisisresponse.com**, and
- a Code of Ethical & Professional Standards.

Membership

Membership with The American Academy of Experts in Traumatic Stress demonstrates a commitment to the field. It is the first step in a sequential process aimed at identifying expertise among professionals across disciplines. There are four levels of membership in the Academy:

- **Member**

  Members must hold a Doctorate in their field of expertise or hold a Masters Degree and have a minimum of three (3) years experience working with survivors of traumatic events. The Executive Officers reserve the right to grant membership to an individual who does not meet the aforementioned criteria, but who has made important contributions to the field or to the Academy.

- **Associate Member**

  This non-doctoral level of membership is reserved for individuals who have at least two (2) years experience working with survivors of traumatic events. Associate Members are afforded all benefits of membership with the exception of qualifying for the Diplomate credential. However, qualified Associate Members may apply for other Academy certifications.

- **Diplomate**

  Members of the Academy may apply for the designation Board Certified Expert in Traumatic Stress—Diplomate, American Academy of Experts in Traumatic Stress.

  To achieve this credential, a comprehensive application and examination, along with supporting documentation, are utilized in concert to validate a member's experience working with survivors of traumatic events, knowledge of the literature and level of education. The Diplomate credential establishes a much needed standard for professionals, across disciplines, who regularly work with survivors of traumatic events. It is the aim of the Academy to have all of our qualified members achieve Diplomate status.

- **Fellow**

  Fellowship is the highest honor the Academy can bestow upon a member. This designation is awarded to Diplomates who have made significant contributions to the field and to the Academy.

Continuing Education Credits

The Academy awards eight (8) continuing education credits to those members who successfully complete the application/examination process leading to Board Certification and the Diplomate Credential. Additionally, six (6) credits are also awarded to those credentialed experts who complete the evaluative process leading to Fellowship with the Academy.

Publications

Trauma Response®, *Trauma Response® Infosheets™* and *Trauma Response® E-News* are the official publications of the Academy. *Trauma Response®* and *Trauma Response® Infosheets™* offer members, from diverse specialties, the opportunity to have articles peer reviewed and published.

Certification in Acute Traumatic Stress Management (ATSM)

Certification is awarded to emergency responders who successfully complete the *Application & Examination for Certification in Acute Traumatic Stress Management*. The examination is based on *Comprehensive Acute Traumatic Stress Management™* published by the Academy.

Certification Programs in Traumatic Stress Specialties

All qualified Members and Associate Members of the Academy will have the opportunity to pursue the following credentials:

Board Certification in Forensic Traumatology™

Board Certification in Emergency Crisis Response™

Board Certification in Motor Vehicle Trauma™

Board Certification in Disability Trauma™

Board Certification in Pain Management™

Board Certification in Illness Trauma™

Board Certification in Bereavement Trauma™

Board Certification in Domestic Violence™

Board Certification in Sexual Abuse™

Board Certification in Rape Trauma™

Board Certification in Stress Management™

Board Certification in School Crisis Response™

These programs require candidates to demonstrate extensive knowledge, experience and education specific to each certification area.

The International Registry

All members in good standing are listed in *The International Registry of The American Academy of Experts in Traumatic Stress*™, the association's official directory and referral network. Members who have achieved Board Certification are listed as credentialed experts in the field. The registry is available in bound copy and can also be accessed directly through the Academy's award winning "guest quarters" on the Internet at **www.aaets.org**.

Credentials

The following are examples of the correct use of The American Academy of Experts in Traumatic Stress' credentials:

- A Member may present his/her status as:
  Robert J. Miller, M.D.
  Member, American Academy of Experts in Traumatic Stress
  Listed in The International Registry of The American Academy of Experts
  in Traumatic Stress

- A Board Certified Expert — Diplomate may use the following credentials:
  Robert J. Miller, M.D., B.C.E.T.S.
  Board Certified Expert in Traumatic Stress
  Diplomate, American Academy of Experts in Traumatic Stress
  Listed in The International Registry of The American Academy of Experts
  in Traumatic Stress

- A Fellow (who has achieved Board Certification) may use the following credentials:
  Robert J. Miller, M.D., B.C.E.T.S., F.A.A.E.T.S.
  Board Certified Expert in Traumatic Stress
  Fellow, American Academy of Experts in Traumatic Stress
  Listed in The International Registry of The American Academy of Experts
  in Traumatic Stress

Members, Associate Members, Diplomates and Fellows who have achieved additional certifications with the Academy in a specialty area may identify themselves with the appropriate credential (e.g., Board Certified in Forensic Traumatology, Board Certified in Emergency Crisis Response, etc.). These professionals may additionally use the respective Academy Credentials, after their educational degree (e.g., Ph.D., B.C.F.T.) or other primary certification (e.g., E.M.T., B.C.E.C.R.), denoting their achievement of specific Academy certifications.

Code of Ethical & Professional Standards

As a multidisciplinary group of professionals, the Academy established a Code of Ethical & Professional Standards for practice across disciplines. All members must adhere to the code.

As a member of The American Academy of Experts in Traumatic Stress, I pledge:

- To be committed to the advancement of intervention for survivors of trauma.

- To maintain the highest standards of competence and professional practice in my work with trauma victims.

- To provide only those services for which I am qualified by virtue of my knowledge, experience and education.

- To maintain my knowledge of the research literature directly related to the services I render.

- To respect the rights of individuals to privacy and confidentiality.

- To never misrepresent my credentials, education or membership status.

- To refrain from conduct that would be adverse to the interest and purpose of the Academy.

- To work toward increasing awareness of traumatic stress and improving intervention with survivors.

Excerpts from *Trauma Response*® Profiles

"The American Academy of Experts in Traumatic Stress fosters awareness. As Sir Francis Bacon said, 'Information is Power.' If we are aware that there is a problem, then there will be people motivated to address the problem. The Academy additionally fosters discovery, innovation, creativity and advancement. And I think that an organization like the Academy helps us strive for raising, to some degree shall I say, the level of quality assurance in the field while promoting creativity and innovation—all with the ultimate goal of being able to better serve people in need."

George S. Everly, Jr., Ph.D., B.C.E.T.S., F.A.A.E.T.S.
Founder & Senior Representative to the United Nations for
the International Critical Incident Stress Foundation

"Being an eclectic group is a very great strength because it allows for a cross-pollination of strategies that have been effective in different disciplines.... The Academy has brought together the best and the brightest to work on better understanding of what it is that occurs during traumatic stress and how to advance clinical applications."

Francine Shapiro, Ph.D., B.C.E.T.S.
Originator & Developer of EMDR

"The Academy is a good forum for a variety of professionals to show people (i.e., survivors of traumatic events) that they can cope with the worst kind of adversity or trauma and not upset themselves about it. Now, people in the field who have some "know-how" in working with trauma can be located in the Academy's International Registry—I think that is a good idea."

Albert Ellis, Ph.D., B.C.E.T.S., F.A.A.E.T.S.
Founder, Albert Ellis Institute

"The Academy is a place to go to obtain and share information, and network with others in a multidisciplinary fashion. When I look at The Academy's Board of Advisors and membership, the only word that comes to mind is eclectic and this organization has certainly covered all the bases.... Also, Trauma Response® *is outstanding and I believe that every one of the Academy's members looks forward to receiving it."*

James T. Reese, Ph.D., B.C.E.T.S., F.A.A.E.T.S.
President, James T. Reese & Associates

"The American Academy of Experts in Traumatic Stress serves a unique and vital purpose. We have to take traumatic stress out of the exclusive domain of psychology and psychiatry. We have to do this! Traumatic stress and its aftermath belong to all of us—medical doctors, lawyers, police departments, psychologists, psychiatrists, teachers, insurance companies, legislators, etc. Education is a crucial step and the issues must be addressed in a public forum."

Beverly J. Anderson, Ph.D., B.C.E.T.S.
President, American Academy of Police Psychology

"Providing an umbrella organization that facilitates dialogue is a valuable service. What the physician, the emergency worker and the psychotherapist have in common and how interventions can be coordinated across disciplines is important. Such a dialogue should result in better treatments for survivors and for those who provide such services."

Donald Meichenbaum, Ph.D.
Clinical Psychologist

"The Academy is multidisciplinary and facilitates different professions coming together under one umbrella. I think that's a great virtue. The cross-pollination that comes from that kind of interaction can only begin to generate a deeper understanding of the phenomenon of traumatic stress as it affects victims and survivors of trauma from all kinds of experience. The Academy provides the opportunity to bring together efforts which allow us to define a mission that transcends ourselves. And in that sense, the Academy, with its diverse and international membership, provides a forum for education, training, publication, and consultation. This not only becomes a national priority or national opportunity, it becomes a potentially global priority of internetting experts in traumatic stress. And I can't think of many things more exciting from my perspective than trying to actualize those objectives which are readily achievable given our technological capacities."

John P. Wilson, Ph.D., B.C.E.T.S., F.A.A.E.T.S.
Founding Member and Past
President of the International
Society for Traumatic Stress Studies

"One of the Academy's major contributions has to do with the fact that this field is so much bigger than any of the individuals in it. To achieve great things, we need to join resources together and have a multidisciplinary approach. Instead of competing, we need to cooperate. Working together, I think we have greater potential to make a larger impact. No one will listen to a small organization with a few members, but when you have a large organization that cuts across the boundaries of many, many professions, then politicians will listen, governments will listen, the citizens will listen, perhaps a serious difference can be made rather than trying to do this all by one's self. I just don't think it's a good idea to work alone in this field—we need to be allied with one another and assist one another in making progress to do something to mitigate the impact of traumatic stress in people's lives."

Jeffrey T. Mitchell, Ph.D.
President, International Critical Incident Stress Foundation

*Committed to the Advancement of Intervention
for Survivors of Trauma*

The American Academy of Experts in Traumatic Stress®
368 Veterans Memorial Hwy., Commack, NY 11725 • Tel. (631) 543-2217 • Fax (631) 543-6977 • www.aaets.org